TOTAL TRUST
In God's Safe Embrace

Catherine J. Duggan

ISBN: 9798844580666

I dedicate this book to my husband Tony and my parents, Pierre & Maureen Desilets. Tony, I am so grateful we get to share this journey called life together. I love you Always & Forever. Mom & Dad, I am forever grateful that you raised us Catholic. You have led by example my whole life. You have both been such powerful witnesses to the our faith. I love you!

Contents

INTRODUCTION

Do you long for a deeper, more intimate relationship with our heavenly Father? I wrote this book because I wanted to help people learn different ways to achieve this very goal. Think of this book as a buffet of ideas that can help you on your quest to deepen your relationship with God. Read through the book and see which options speak to you. Most likely some will speak to you more than others. Just try the ones you are interested in trying.

My advice would be to just start with one new thing. More times than I can count, I have read about different ways I could increase my faith and I decide to add several things at a time. For instance, I can say the Rosary each day, which takes only 20 minutes. I could also say this novena, which only takes 3 minutes. Then, before bed, I could do some prayer journaling to review my day. While it may be true that these things just take a few minutes, they all start to add up to quite a bit of time. It also can become overwhelming. This is because now I have three new habits I need to remember to do every day. For me, if I add just one new thing to my life at a time, I am a lot more successful.

This book promises to give you 15 things you could do to increase your faith and develop a more intimate relationship with our Lord. I will not only tell you about my experience with each one, I will explain how to do them and the benefits you will get from them. You may not be interested in all 15 ideas. There may be some that just aren't for you. That is great, no worries. If you pick one thing from this book to do regularly, you will see an increase in your faith. The wonderful thing about spirituality, is that there are so many different ways to express it. This book describes the things that worked for me. Many other things work for other people. If you read this whole book and do not feel as though any of these will work for you, I would say two things: First, pick one and try it for 30 days. If it does nothing for you, then move on. It's hard to know if something works without giving it a try. Second, don't stop looking. There is so much out there, find something that you can do regularly to help you increase your faith. You won't be sorry that you did.

There isn't just one path to build a closer relationship with the Lord. There are many different paths and you get to take the one that feels best for you. The Catholic Church, for instance, has many different traditions, prayers, saints, devotions, etc. Many different groups/organizations focus on one aspect for spiritual growth or another. Do not worry about picking the one right devotion or saying that one right prayer. Your journey to holiness is very personal and individual. What speaks to me may not speak to you. It may take a little trial and error to see what works for you.

Many different religious orders of men and women dedicated their lives to God in very different ways. Some groups of religious sisters, such at the Carmelite nuns and Poor Clares, are cloistered. Being cloistered means they stay at their monastery and do not venture out into the world. They stay within the boundaries of the monastery unless there is an emergency. While in the monastery, these women search daily for the face of God.

Then you have Mother Teresa's mission, which was to serve the sick people of Calcutta. She went into the streets and found the people that no one else would help. She sat with them in their final hours. She washed their wounds and opened hospitals to take care of them. Her approach to holiness was very different than the cloistered nuns.

Many religious orders start by following the path that certain saints took to follow God. For instance, Franciscan religious orders follow St. Francis's path. St. Ignatius of Loyola came up with some very specific spiritual exercises that some orders dedicate their lives to following. They try to live as he lived.

There are many different things that you can do to increase your faith. There are so many different paths, or devotions that you could follow. However, it is impossible to follow ALL these paths! There are so many wonderful traditions and devotions or prayers or saints to follow, that I have gotten caught trying to do too many things at once. For instance, some believe that saying St. Gertrude's prayer releases 1,000 souls from Purgatory. I immediately wanted to add this to my daily routine. I mean it only takes a minute or two. Then there is the Liturgy of the Hours. This is a group of prayers put together to say throughout the day. I thought that would be great and wouldn't take too long. Do you see where I am going with this? There is so much from which to choose and it is ALL really good. Each option is relatively easy and would take just a few minutes out of your day. However, start adding 10 quick things to your day, and it is no longer just a few extra minutes.

This book is not intended to make you feel guilty about the things you could be doing that you are not doing. I am a big believer in Grace. We could all probably be better with prayer or putting God first. However, we should not beat ourselves up about something that we can't change. Instead, we should be graceful with ourselves and move on. It is not too late to start a daily prayer habit, to begin reading spiritual books, or to say a Rosary.

I hope that you find at least one thing in this book that speaks to you as a way to increase your faith and deepen your relationship with God. We all have different likes and interests. The 15 ways presented in this book increased my faith and trust in God over the last 16 years. If you read them all and do not find one that speaks to you or sparks an interest in you, then I pray that you will continue to search for what works best for you. An infinite number of ways exist to deepen your relationship with God and to increase your faith. Take the time to figure out how you can spend at least 10 minutes a day with God. You will not be sorry.

CHAPTER ONE

The Power of Daily Prayer

Daily prayer is something that I have strived to achieve for many years. I would try to spend time praying each day, but I was not really sure how. I would wonder if writing in my journal counted, or if me praying for a parking spot, or for my child to fall asleep and take a nap counted as prayer time for the day. I was so unsure and afraid to get it wrong. Have you ever felt that way? I can't be the only person that has been afraid of praying wrong. If I could go back, I would tell my younger self, yes, all those prayers counted. I would tell myself that God is not sitting up there judging my prayers, He is happy that I took the time out of my day to talk with him. Your prayers are never wasted. It is not as if some count and some don't. God hears all of our prayers.

If you are looking to deepen your relationship with God, a daily practice of prayer is essential. This can be accomplished in many different ways. This section tells you about how I got started on my prayer journey. I will give you several examples of things I tried and ways you could develop a daily prayer habit. Sometimes we get so caught up in telling ourselves we don't know how to pray, that we never start trying to develop the habit of daily prayer.

Prayer was part of my life ever since I can remember. When I was young, my mom or dad would come to my room at night and say prayers with me. We said the same prayer every night as far as I can recall. "Dear God, please bless my mother and father, my brothers and sisters, my aunts and uncles, and my cousins and friends." Sometimes we would add, "please also bless everyone we know and everyone we don't know." This was a very simple prayer and yet it covered everyone. If you are wondering why we did not name our brothers and sisters, aunts and uncles or cousins, it was because I come from a very large family. There are 11 children in my family and my mother was the oldest of 10 children. If we named everyone, I would have never gotten to sleep.

Growing up Catholic, prayer was also part of Mass. We say many of the same prayers at Mass every week and so we have plenty of opportunity to learn several prayers to use even when we are outside of Mass. These prayers were our staple and it felt great to have them when we wanted to pray. If someone asks you to pray for them, a Hail Mary or an Our Father is an excellent choice. However, these prayers did not give us room to personalize them. I would hear other people come up with a prayer off the top of their head and I thought that was amazing. Also, when people would say grace and it was personal and individualized, I loved it. I wished I knew how to do that.

I know there is no right or wrong way to pray. The definition for prayer is the following: Prayer- a solemn request for help or expression of thanks addressed to God or an object of worship. So, if we are just requesting something from God or expressing our thanks, how can there be a right or wrong way to pray? Do you wonder, when you are saying thanks to your friend, if you said it the right way? I doubt it. Do you question if you requested your combo meal from the fast food worker correctly? Nope. Then why do we question how to pray? I ask this as much to myself as to you.

Until about a year, ago I felt really uncomfortable praying out loud, unless it was a prayer I had memorized, like the Our Father. Two years ago I joined a charismatic prayer group, and I remember the first time they asked us to put our hand on our neighbor's shoulder and pray over that person. I felt bad for the person I was praying over because they had me praying over them. I felt like I was not good enough to pray over them and someone else's prayers would be better. This may sound silly, but I bet many of you know exactly what I was feeling that day. Why do we struggle so much with wanting to say the right thing? I take comfort in knowing that I am not the only one that feels as though I do not know how to pray. Even the disciples, who were in the presence of Jesus, were unsure of how to pray. In Luke 11:1-4 "One day Jesus was praying in a certain place. When he finished, one of his disciples said to him, 'Lord, teach us to pray, just as John taught his disciples.' He said to them,"When you pray, say: 'Father, hallowed be your name, your kingdom come. Give us each day our daily bread. Forgive us our sins, for we also forgive everyone who sins against us. And lead us not into temptation.'"

I have been listening to people pray out loud at my prayer group for two years now and I realized everyone prays differently. There is not just one way to pray. There is no secret prayer formula to which God listens more closely. Do you ever feel like God hears other people's prayers more than he hears yours? Is it just me? In my family we always say that my dad's prayers go straight to heaven. We think that because he prays more often God hears his prayers more than ours. He is a prayer giant and I am sure you know someone who is. The truth is, God always listens. He listens to everyone's prayers, not just those who pray every day. In 1 John 5:14 John says, " This is the confidence we have in approaching God: that if we ask anything according to his will, **he hears us**." John goes on to say in 1 John 5:15, "And if we know that he hears us, whatsoever we ask, we know that we have the petitions that we desired of him." God hears your prayers, even if your prayers are not eloquent, or too short, or non specific.—He hears you!

Having said all that, do not expect to suddenly feel comfortable praying just because someone told you there is no right or wrong way to pray. I wanted to explain some of the ways I started my prayer habit. I urge you to choose one of these and start your new prayer habit today. If you are already in the habit of praying every day, great! If you want to try something new, that's great too. Most importantly, spend at least 10 minutes with God each and every day. You will begin to see a difference.

To start you can:

Write in a prayer journal. Write down what you want to pray for, or how your day was. I started this when I was struggling and sometimes it would just be me expressing to God my hurts, my confusions, and/or my struggles. Other times I would request help for others or myself. Sometimes I would just thank Him for all He has done. It was all very conversational; I started as if I was writing Him a letter. I initially started with "Dear Lord." Now I start with Good Morning, Dad." (More about prayer journaling in the next chapter)

Pray with people when they ask you for prayers. People are always asking for prayers. Instead of saying that I will pray for them later, I started praying for them right there on the spot. Yes, I felt uncomfortable, and yes, I felt like I was doing it wrong. Then I reminded myself that there is no wrong way and that no one was judging me. I believe God loves it when we step out in faith and step outside our comfort zone to show His love to others. The only way to grow is to step outside your comfort zone and try something new. Just start with asking God for whatever the person needs. For instance, "Dear Heavenly Father, please help my friend in the meeting with her boss today. Please give her the courage and wisdom she needs to say the things she needs to say." It could be that simple. Just a quick prayer that is asking for whatever is needed at the time.

Read the Bible more. When you immerse yourself in God's word, the words to pray over people come more easily. It is easier to call on God's promises to us, because you know what God promises. If you have tried to read the Bible and just could not get through it, try again and start with the gospels? They are more like stories than some of the Old Testament books. Father Mike Schmitz just started a podcast where he will read The Bible on the podcast in one year. This could be a great option if you have a commute. You could use this time to hear The Bible. He not only reads it, but he explains it in terms that make it easier to understand.

Pray before meals. When the boys were little and they went to a Christian pre-school, they were given a few different versions of prayers to say before meals. I printed them and put a magnet on the back of them. Each night one of the boys would pick one off the fridge and that would be the prayer we said that night. Most of the time now, we say the main one that I have heard lots of people say: "Bless us oh Lord, and these thy gifts, which we are about to receive from thy bounty through Christ our Lord, Amen." It doesn't have to be complicated. You could just take a second and say "Thank you, God, for this food."

Say the Rosary daily. This takes about 20-30 minutes and can be a very powerful way to start a prayer habit. (More about the Rosary in chapter 3)

Spend 10 minutes each day talking with God, out loud or in your head. I used to do this when I was alone in my car driving somewhere. I would just start talking with God about my day, my wants, my needs, any prayer requests I had.

These are just a few things you could do to start praying more or start praying differently. I hope you find them helpful. Whenever I am praying or trying to serve God and I think I may do it wrong or I may not be good enough, I think of a word that came to someone at one of my prayer group meetings:

"My children, I love you to be with me. I do not need your efforts; I do not need your talents, for I alone will make you fruitful. Just relax, be empty and be with me."

God does not need us to say the right thing, He just wants us to come to Him and to be with Him. He will make your prayers fruitful. Our efforts or talents do not provide answers to our prayers, it is by the grace and goodness of God.

Following is a quote by St. Alphonsus Liguori, which I believe embodies the best way to pray.

"Acquire the habit of speaking with God as if you were alone with Him, familiarly and with confidence and love as to the dearest and most loving of friends."

Just have a conversation with God as you would your best friend.

CHAPTER TWO

The Power of a Prayer Journal

For Christmas in 2005 my uncle Jeano gave me a notebook. Inside the notebook was a letter from him that explained all about spiritual journaling/prayer journaling. I had never done prayer journaling before and my first thought was that it was for people who were holier than me. I am sure you can start to see this recurring theme in my thoughts. I tend to feel like I am not holy enough to do all these different things. I am not sure why it took so long to realize these ideas could be a path to becoming more holy. In the letter, my uncle listed four benefits to prayer journaling. These are:

- Deepening your relationship with God.
- Helping you to see God really does answer your prayers as you look back and see it in your own writing time after time.
- Increasing your confidence (in God) as you take things to Him in your Journal.
- Having someone to go to and unload on, anytime, anywhere, who can truly "handle it."

All of that sounded amazing. I was always looking for some way to deepen my relationship with God. "What if I do it wrong?" "What if I say the wrong thing?" These questions popped into my head. I decided to try it anyway. What is the worse that can happen, right? I made my first entry on January 11, 2006. This is how I began my first entry, "I've written in a journal before, but not regularly, and not a prayer journal. I don't know if there are certain rules, but I will just write what I am thinking. I am sure I will get better and more focused with practice." Then I started to write about my day. That first day I wrote four pages in my new journal. I was so excited to start this new practice and I felt great afterwards.

I would love to say that from that day on I spent 10-20 minutes a day writing to God in that journal. Unfortunately, that was not the case. I just took out that journal to check how often I wrote in it, as I remembered it wasn't often. It turns out after that first entry, on January 11, 2006, my next entry is on June 4, 2010. What?! I did not write in my prayer journal again for another 4 years. In case you had any illusions that I have it all figured out and this spiritual stuff came easier to me, I don't and it didn't. I wrote in my journal for a few days in June and then not again until September. Then it was once in September, once in October, and once in December. Just to give you an idea of how inconsistent my journaling was, my journal had 44 pages and it took me until June 2017 to fill it.

In Spring of 2017 I attended a retreat sponsored by the Military Council of Catholic Women (MCCW). I am not sure exactly what was said at this retreat to give me this conviction, but I came home from the retreat with the conviction that I needed to turn to God for help with my family issues. I struggled with parenting our three boys, as they were very strong willed, and Tony and I could not seem to get on the same page. Our marriage was also struggling.

I had read almost every parenting book out there, as well as many marriage books. A thought came to me at the retreat, that I was looking everywhere but to God for answers. I wrestled with this thought because I had been praying to him all along the way. What I heard in response to my question was I was spending more time trying to come up with my own answers than I was spending time trying to hear God's answers to my prayers. Wow, that was not what I was expecting to hear.

When I got home from this retreat, I made a resolution to get up before the kids each morning and write in my prayer journal. Write to Him and let Him know all that was going on in my life.

I know that He already knows what is going on, but it's nice when we make time to talk with Him about it. You may know that your child went outside to play on the playground, but wouldn't you still love to hear them explain what they did out there in their own words?

Talk to God about your day, your wins, your struggles, and anything else you want to talk to him about. I believe it makes God happy when we make time to talk with Him. He is our Father, and He wants to talk with His children. I got up almost every morning after that retreat and wrote in a journal. I talked about my day and what things were going on in our family. I thanked God for whatever I could and I asked for help in the areas I needed help in. I was so thankful I was able to have the discipline to get up early each morning and do this. It was such a change from my past attempts, from June 2017-Sept. 2017 I filled a whole journal.

I felt a great sense of peace while I was writing in the journal daily. I did feel my relationship with God deepening. It is similar to having a best friend you can talk to every day. I have heard from many sources that writing is good for your soul. Think how much better for your soul it is when you are writing to your heavenly father.

There are many different techniques to prayer journal and I have tried a few different ones. While writing this chapter I looked back at some of my journals and was reminded of the different formats I have used. There is no right or wrong way to start a prayer journal. You can just get a notebook and start writing. I hope you do that. My wish for you is to get a notebook, any notebook and just start writing. The only reason I am writing this part is because I know I like to have directions. I like to have an example of at least one way someone else did it so I can get started. If I am just told to do something without an example, sometimes I get stuck trying to decide how to start and I never start.

The first type of journaling I did was just writing whatever came to my mind. I would write as if I was talking to someone sitting next to me. I would write about my day, or what I did the day before. I would write about what I had coming up that day or anything I needed prayers for. I would also list any prayer requests I had received from others.

If I happened to be struggling with anything, and let's be real, I always was, then I would talk about that and ask for God's help. I would ask for His wisdom in a certain circumstance, or His patience, or strength to make it through. Whatever I felt I needed on that particular day, or in that particular circumstance. Sometimes I would write for a few pages, and sometimes I would fall asleep after writing a paragraph. It doesn't matter. I truly believe that God loves our desire for holiness and He loves any attempt at trying to grow closer to him.

The next type of journaling I learned from Dynamic Catholic. I have received it on a prayer card with most of my orders. Also, the description is in the book, The *Four Signs of a Dynamic Catholic* by Matthew Kelly. Here is the prayer process from Dynamic Catholic:

1. Gratitude: Begin by thanking God in a personal dialogue for whatever you are most grateful for today.
2. Awareness: Revisit the times in the past twenty-four hours when you were and were not the-best-version-of-yourself. Talk to God about these situations and what you learned from them.
3. Significant Moments: Identify something you experienced today and explore what God might be trying to say to you through that event (or person).
4. Peace: Ask God to forgive you for any wrong you have committed (against yourself, another person, or Him) and to fill you with a deep and abiding peace.
5. Freedom: Speak with God about how He is inviting you to change your life, so that you can experience the freedom to be the-best-version-of-yourself.
6. Others: Lift up to God anyone you can feel called to pray for today, asking God to bless and guide them.
7. Finish by praying the Our Father.

I would look at my day and go through these 6 steps in my journal. Sometimes it would just be a sentence for each one, sometimes it would be longer. I think it is important to note that in step two it says to notice where **you were** and **were not** the best version of yourself. I think when we look back over our day it may be easy to think about all the times we might have missed the mark. Especially if we are a spouse or parent, we can usually see all the places throughout the day when we could have been better. Maybe we yelled at our children or lost our temper with our spouse. I think it's important to examine these and see how we might be able to respond better next time.

However, I feel it is just as important to look at the things we did right today. How many times did we want to yell, but didn't? Did we go outside and play with our child even though we really wanted to stay inside and read a book? If we only focus on the negative we may start to feel like all we do is mess up. However, when we are also looking at the things we did right we see we are not the terrible person we thought we were. If we know we are doing some things right, we can try to increase the number of times we get it right and decrease the number of times we get it wrong.

A third type of journaling I did came from the book called Consoling the Heart of Jesus by Father Michael E. Gaitley.[1] He presented this method as an Examination of Conscience. I went through these steps before bed, and I wrote them in my journal during this period of journaling. You would begin by putting yourself in the presence of God. Then follow the steps in the acronym B. A. K. E. R.

- B = Blessings. Spend the most time here, praising and thanking God for the blessing of the day.
- A = Ask. Ask the Holy Spirit to enlighten you, so you can recognize your sins.
- K = Kill. It was our sins that killed and crucified Jesus. Search for commissions and omissions. (This means what did you do that you shouldn't have done and what didn't you do that you should have done.)
- E = Embrace. Be sorry for sin and allow Jesus to embrace

---

[1] "Used with permission of the Marian Fathers of the Immaculate Conception of the B. V. M."

you with rays of his mercy.

- R = Resolution. Look ahead to the next day, anticipating potential pitfalls and opportunities.

I would think about each step and write the things that came to mind. I would think about all of my blessings for that day, all the things I had to be grateful for, and I would write them down. (B) Then I would write in my journal (although you could just say it), "Holy Spirit, come down and show me my sins," or "Holy Spirit, show me all the ways I have sinned today." (A) Then I would write down anything that comes to mind. (K) For the next step I would tell God I was sorry for my sins and ask Him for His help to keep me from sinning again. (E). Next, I would picture God's rays of mercy shining down on me. Finally, I would think about the following day and write down one thing I could do to help it go more smoothly and to be a better version of myself. Just that intentional few minutes of planning I found to be very helpful.

Another way a lot of people use their prayer journal is to read a Bible verse or chapter and then talk to God in their journal about what the verse said to them. They explain what it meant to them, or what they thought of when they read it. Maybe you could relate that scripture to whatever you are going through on that particular day. I think you would be surprised how the same scripture verse can speak to you differently depending on what you are experiencing at the time. You could also read a daily devotional, you don't have to buy a book, they have some online. After you read the daily devotional you could write your reactions to it in your journal. Also, some devotionals have questions at the end of them. You could answer these during you journaling time.

Hopefully, these examples show you the there are many different ways to do your prayer journaling. I have used many of them at one time or another. Currently, I am writing a letter to God each day. I begin the letter with "Hi Dad," "Good Morning, Father," or some variation of this. I did not feel comfortable when I started referring to God as Dad as it felt informal and even disrespectful. However, He is our Dad and I believe He longs for a deep and intimate relationship with us, so I have grown comfortable with addressing my letters in this manner. You may not, and again that is great. We are all on our own journey. No two journeys will be the same. God made us perfectly equipped for our own journey. You know what you feel comfortable with and what you don't. He loves you because you are you, not because you are trying to be like someone else. Just be yourself, write from the heart and I bet He will love it!

CHAPTER THREE

Powerful Prayers for Your Journey

I have found a number of structured prayers that have really helped strengthen my faith. The first of these is the Rosary. When I moved to New Jersey, one of the wives in Tony's squadron had started a home Rosary group. I did not know what that even meant, but I had just moved to a new place and I did not know anyone. I knew I needed something more, as I had a newborn baby and was just learning how to be a mom.

A home Rosary group is a group of people that gather at someone's home and say the Rosary together. Our group met once a week, but each group can decide how often they want to meet. One person leads either the whole Rosary, or leaders switch for each decade (a decade is a series of 10 Hail Marys), whichever you prefer. Whoever leads the Rosary says the first half of the prayer and then everyone says the second half of the prayer. It was so nice to be gathered with a group of women who wanted to say the Rosary each week.

If you do not know what the Rosary is, or how to begin to say the Rosary, you are not alone. The Rosary is a group of Roman Catholic prayers you say, usually using a set of Rosary beads. The back of this book includes instructions about how to say the Rosary.

I have always found the Rosary to be very powerful. However, don't take my word for it. While researching for this book, I found 15 Promises that The Blessed Virgin Mary gave to Saint Dominic. Mary promised that "Whatever you ask in the Rosary will be granted." She left these promises for all Christians who recite the Holy Rosary. They were imparted to Saint Dominic and Blessed Alan. The Rosary only takes about 20-30 minutes a day and yet saying it can benefit you in so many incredible ways. Saying the Rosary takes less time than watching one episode on Hulu or Netflix. What would you give up during your day, or once a week in order to have any of these promises in your life?

Here are the 15 Promises:

1. Whoever shall faithfully serve me by the recitation of the Rosary, **shall receive signal graces.**

2. I promise my **special protection** and the **greatest graces** to all those who shall recite the Rosary.

3. The Rosary shall be a **powerful armor against hell**, it will **destroy vice, decrease sin,** and **defeat heresies**.

4. The Rosary will **cause virtue** and good works to flourish; it will obtain for souls the **abundant mercy of God**; it will **withdraw the hearts of men from the love of the world and its vanities**, and will **lift them to the desire for eternal things**. Oh, that souls would sanctify themselves by this means.

5. The soul which recommends itself to me by the recitation of the Rosary, **shall not perish**.

6. Whoever shall recite the Rosary devoutly, applying himself to the consideration of its sacred mysteries shall **never be conquered by misfortune**. God will not chastise him in His justice, he shall not perish by an unprovided death; if he be just **he shall remain in the grace of God**, and become **worthy of eternal life**.

7. Whoever shall have a true devotion for the Rosary **shall not die without the sacraments** of the Church.

8. Those who are faithful to recite the Rosary shall have **during their life and at their death the light of God** and the **plenitude of His graces**; at the moment of death they **shall participate in the merits of the saints** in paradise.

9. I shall **deliver from Purgatory** those **who have been devoted to the Rosary**.

10. The faithful children of the Rosary shall **merit a high**

degree of glory in Heaven.

11. You shall **obtain all you ask** of me **by the recitation of the Rosary**.

12. All those who **propagate the Holy Rosary** shall be **aided by me in their necessities**.

13. I have obtained from my Divine Son that all the **advocates of the Rosary shall have for intercessors the entire celestial court during their life and at the hour of death.**

14. All **who recite the Rosary** are my sons and daughters, and brothers and sisters of my only Son Jesus Christ.

15. Devotion of my Rosary is a **great sign of predestination**.

Another really helpful prayer is the Chaplet of Divine Mercy. This chaplet is another group of prayers you can say using Rosary beads. You say different prayers on each bead. Directions about how to say the Chaplet of Divine Mercy appear in the back of this book.

The history of this chaplet is amazing. Saint Faustina Kowalska was a nun in Poland. She received a vision that an angel was sent by God to chastise a certain city. She immediately began to pray for mercy, but no matter how much she prayed for mercy, she could not save the city.

Then she saw the Holy Trinity and felt the power of Jesus' grace within her. At the same time she found herself praying words that she heard internally, "Eternal Father, I offer You the Body and Blood, Soul and Divinity of Your dearly beloved Son, Our Lord Jesus Christ, in atonement for our sins and those of the whole world; for the sake of His sorrowful Passion, have mercy on us." (*Saint Faustina's Diary*, 475)

As she continued saying this inspired prayer, the angel became helpless and could not carry out the deserved punishment (see 474). The next day, as she was entering the chapel, she again heard this interior voice, instructing her how to recite the prayer our Lord later called "the Chaplet." This time, after "have mercy on us" were added the words "and on the whole world" (476). From then on, she recited this form of prayer almost constantly, offering it especially for the dying.

Our Lord made many promises attached to the praying of the Chaplet of Divine Mercy, which were revealed in *The Diary of St. Faustina Kowalska*. The chaplet takes about 10 minutes. What is it in your day or your week that you could replace with this prayer? **Here are those promises:**[2]

1. "I promise that the soul that will venerate this image (of Divine Mercy) will not perish. I also promise victory over (its) enemies already here on earth, especially at the hour of death. I Myself will defend it as My own glory." (Diary, 48)

2. "The souls that say this chaplet will be embraced by My mercy during their lifetime and especially at the hour of their death." (Diary, 754)

3. "When hardened sinners say it, I will fill their souls with peace, and the hour of their death will be a happy one." (Diary, 1541)

4. "When they say this chaplet in the presence of the dying, I will stand between My Father and the dying person, not as a just Judge but as a merciful Savior." (Diary, 1541)

5. "Whoever will recite it will receive great mercy at the hour of death." (Diary, 687)

6. "Priests will recommend it to sinners as their last hope of salvation. Even if there were a sinner most hardened, if he were to recite this chaplet only once, he would receive grace from My infinite mercy...I desire to grant unimaginable graces to those souls who trust in My mercy." (Diary, 687)

7. "To priests who proclaim and extol My mercy, I will give wondrous power; I will anoint their words and touch the hearts of those to whom they will speak." (Diary, 1521)

8. "The prayer most pleasing to Me is prayer for the conversion for sinners. Know, my daughter, that this prayer is always heard and answered." (Diary, 1397)

9. "At three o'clock, implore My mercy, especially for sinners; and, if only for a brief moment, immerse yourself

---

[2] "Used with permission of the Marian Fathers of the Immaculate Conception of the B. V. M."

in My Passion, particularly in My abandonment at the moment of agony...I will refuse nothing to the soul that makes a request of Me in virtue of My Passion." (Diary, 1320; also, cf. Diary, 1572)

10. "Souls who spread the honor of My mercy...at the hour of death I will not be a Judge for them, but the Merciful Savior." (Diary, 1075)

11. "The two rays denote Blood and Water...These two rays issued from the very depths of My tender mercy when My agonized Heart was opened by a lance on the Cross. These rays shield souls from the wrath of My Father...I desire that the first Sunday after Easter be the Feast of Mercy...whoever approaches the Fount of Life on this day will be granted complete remission of sins and punishment. Mankind will not have peace until it turns with trust to My mercy." (Diary, 299-300)

12. "I desire that the Feast of Mercy...be solemnly celebrated on the first Sunday after Easter...The soul that will go to Confession and receive Holy Communion (in a state of grace on this day) shall obtain complete forgiveness of sins and punishment." (Diary, 699)

13. "Through this chaplet you will obtain everything, if what you ask for is compatible with My will." (Diary, 1731)

14. "My mercy is greater than your sins and those of the entire world." (Diary, 1485)

I have also found various novenas particularly helpful. A novena is a prayer, or group of prayers, that you say for 9 consecutive days. My mother told me that when she and my father were trying to have a baby, they would say a novena. They had 11 children, so I would say they found novenas particularly fruitful.

There are many different novenas for many different purposes. One novena that is particularly helpful is Mary Undoer of Knots. This is a great one to say when life is especially hard. If you are struggling with family issues, work issues, lack of understanding between parents and children, perhaps the knots of deep hurt between a husband and wife, this is the novena for you. Our

Mother Mary wants to help us. She is just waiting for us to ask.

There is a Miraculous Rosary where you say 3 Rosary novenas (27 days) in petition for something and then you say 3 more Rosary novenas (27 days) in thanksgiving for your petition, even if you have not yet received your answer. It is similar to the regular Rosary, but there are some additional prayers you say with it. I have used this Rosary several times.

Once we were praying for our neighbor's daughter who was in first grade. They found out that she had cancer and might have to lose her leg. We prayed that she would keep her leg and be cured of the cancer. She did have something in her leg removed, but she still has her leg, she can walk on her own, and she no longer has cancer. We are so very thankful. To learn how to say the 54 day miraculous Rosary, see all of the directions and prayers at *www.54daynovena.com*.

I have found so many prayers helpful over the years. I do not have space to list them all in this chapter. I will end with the two I have been saying most recently. At a prayer group meeting one of the ladies challenged us to pray the Litany of Humility every day for a month and see if we felt any different afterwards. Humility is something that is mentioned often and I had prayed for humility numerous times. So I was excited for this challenge. I did not say it every day, but I did do it most days. I definitely noticed a difference. Not only with how I felt, but I was starting to understand the different components of humility. I continued to say this litany almost daily.

One day I wondered if there were litanies for other virtues. I found the Litany of Trust. I started to say this litany almost daily. I found this immensely helpful. Trusting in the Lord is something I have been praying for a lot over the years. I longed for a supernatural trust where I would just know that all would be ok. I prayed for a radical trust, trust that I could pray for something and not doubt if God was going to hear me, or wonder if he was going to answer my prayers.

This prayer helped me to understand different aspects of trust. I said it almost every day for a month or two and then decided to alternate days between praying the Litany of Trust and the Litany of Humility. Since I began the Litany of Trust, my trust in the Lord has grown stronger. There are many things currently happening in my life, as I am sure there are in your life, that test that trust. There are many things I could stress about all day long.

However, I do not spend my days stressed about all the what ifs in the world. I know without a shadow of a doubt that God is looking out for me and those I love. I don't have to worry because I turned all of it over to Him and He wants better for me than I could ever imagine. I know the Litany has helped this trust grow and I am so thankful. Living life in a constant state of worry is not fun for anyone. Worry is the opposite of faith. It robs us of the peace that Christ gives us. If you are anxious, or worry a lot, I suggest you try saying the Litany of Trust every day for a month and see how different you feel afterwards.

CHAPTER FOUR

Powerful Podcasts

At some point in my journey, I was lead to podcasts. I found several I really enjoy. One reason I enjoy podcasts so much is because a new episode comes out each week. One of the podcasts I listen to is actually a daily devotional, but most are released weekly. I also like that they are not usually very long. All the ones I listen to are under an hour. Some are 30-45 minutes and some are 10-20 minutes. The more we surround ourselves with the word of God and our faith, the more we will grow in our faith. Having something new to listen to each week is great!

Another reason I love to listen to podcasts, books, and music about faith, religion, praise and worship is because I love to fill my brain with all that knowledge. Jim Rohn, a motivational speaker, said that we are the average of the five people with whom we spend the most time. With whom do you spend the most time? Are they people who have the beliefs and values that you have or want? Sometimes, we do not get much say about with whom we spend time. We may spend time with co-workers although we do not agree with their beliefs or values. You may spend a lot of time with family members who are negative when you want to be positive.

The reason you are the average of the five people with whom you spend the most time is that you hear their voices, thoughts, and feelings all the time. Have you ever noticed that when you hang around with someone a lot, you start to talk like that person? They may use words you had not even heard before, but because you are around them so often and they say that word so much, you start to use it too.

Sometimes you start to like something you did not like before just because of exposure to it. I heard a story of a guy who was doing a research report on steroids. He was against them. Because he was doing so much research about them, advertisements for steroids starting showing up on his social media. He was annoyed at first, but after seeing them every day, he started to wonder if he should give them a try, even though he was against them in the first place.

You may not have complete control over with whom you spend the most time, but you do have control over what you listen to and with what you choose to surround yourself. If you spend your free time or your commute time listening to things that help you learn more about your faith or help to increase your faith, then those will be the voices and thoughts that play repeatedly in your head. If all you hear are negative voices, either your own or others, you will start to believe those voices.

Following are seven of the podcasts that have helped me grow in faith.

1). The Jeff Cavins Show- Jeff Cavins has a weekly podcast. Each week he discusses a different topic. This podcast is usually about 30 minutes. If you like his Bible studies you will love his podcast. During his podcast, Jeff shares faith tips and scripture truths to help you live as a modern-day disciple of Jesus Christ. One of my favorite episodes is called, "Who's in Your Spiritual Posse?" This was a great episode, Jeff talked about how creating his own personal spiritual posse comprising a group of saints he talks to every single day.

His has his favorite saints are each the patron saint of something he wants to improve in his own life. Each day he begins by greeting the saints. He spends time getting to know them and reads about their lives and the incredible things they did while they were alive. He talks with them all the time. He wears a necklace, with a medal for each of the 5 saints on it, to remind him that his friends are with him always. He prays with them and asks them to intercede on his behalf.

2.) Abiding Together is a podcast hosted by three best friends; Heather Khym, Michelle Benzinger, and Sister Miriam James Heidland. The purpose of this podcast is to provides a place of connection, rest and encouragement for women who are on the journey of living out their passion and purpose in Jesus Christ. Each week they discuss various topics. This podcast is about 45 minutes long. Sometimes the three of them discuss what they think about a certain topic, and other times they interview someone about a particular topic, like Bishop Robert Barron.

They also have book studies. They announce the book ahead of time and each week they discuss what they learned from the book. Because there are three people that host this podcast, you get to see what each one of them learned from the book. I really enjoy this because each one of them has great insight and often different aspects of the book touch them.

Another thing I enjoy about this podcast is you get to join them on their journey to holiness. You hear about their struggles and how they use their struggles to grow. You see how the Lord is moving in their lives and therefore, that it is possible for Him to move in your own life. You can tell by listening to them that their relationships with God are very important to each of them. They are also a great example of how friends can help us on our journey. We should all have friends who love us enough to speak up if we are doing something to hurt our relationship with Jesus.

3.) Your Catholic Life with Jon Leonetti is a podcast that comes out each week. Jon's podcast usually lasts 10-12 minutes. I can listen to a whole episode while I am driving to the grocery store. Jon usually interviews someone different each week. He interviews authors, speakers, and, one time, an NHL All-Star MVP. Each interview is extremely well thought out and very informational. I love how much you can learn in 10 minutes. Jon loves the Catholic Church and the faith. You can tell just by listening to him that he loves God.

4.) Fr. Mike Schmitz Catholic Podcast is about faith, pop culture, and headline reflections. If there are things about the Catholic Church that you do not understand, or that you have always wondered about, he has probably addressed it in one of his podcasts. This podcast is another one that is pretty short. It is generally between 8-10 minutes.

The range of topics is great. He covers everything from "Why are Some People so Annoying," to "The Real Answer to Why God Allows Suffering." I grew up Catholic and so I have been Catholic for a very long time. However, there are still many things that I either did not know, or did not understand. Thanks to this podcast I am learning so much, not only about my faith, but life in general.

5.) The Big Life Devotional with Pamela Crim. This devotional airs every week day and is about 15 minutes long. Monday through Friday you can begin your mornings with Pamela. She has so much energy and also so much love for God and for Life. She begins each podcast with an awesome greeting, "Good Morning Beautiful, and welcome to a brand new day of life." She also ends each episode with, "I love you wildly." You can tell she means it too.

Each morning Pamela gets up early and spends time with the Lord. She has an idea of what she wants to talk about, and she is also open to the Holy Spirit. If He takes her in a whole new direction, she is good with it. I am amazed that so many women can hear the same devotional and all get different messages from it. God definitely works through her to get his message out in the world.

Each devotional is based on a Bible scripture. She takes the normal everyday things that happen to us in life and gives us hope and strength through the scripture verses and her message. She also talks a lot about living a big life, living up to all of the potential that God has placed within us. I love this. I personally don't think people dream enough these days. I believe God created each one of us for an amazing life. Too often we settle into what is comfortable to us and we don't step out in faith to live the life God created us to live.

Listening to Pamela's devotional each day is inspiring and motivational. I love hearing her talk about all the different stories in the Bible. Sometimes, she talks about a passage that most of us might have just passed over - a verse you read, but didn't think much about. Then she does a whole devotional about it and that verse takes on a whole new meaning or significance. She really has an amazing gift.

6.) Elevation with Steven Furtick. This weekly podcast is like a sermon from Pastor Steven Furtick, and is about an hour long. I really enjoy the message in this podcast. Steven has a way of explaining things that make them so easy to understand. He also has a way of stating things that makes you really examine what you are doing and why you are doing it. If you enjoy the Sunday sermons at your church, I am sure you will love this podcast. It is just like a Sunday sermon, but you can listen to it any day of the week.

7.) Exploring My Strange Bible by Tim Mackie. Tim is a pastor at a church in Oregon. He put together a collection of his sermons and teachings on the Bible over a 10-year period and offers them here, all in one place. Each episode is about 45-60 minutes and is like a mini Bible study. I truly enjoy studying the Bible.

It is not always easy to find a Bible study. My church only had one on Thursday mornings, and this is when I had my charismatic prayer group. Even if you are able to find a Bible study, it takes commitment to sign up and go. It also takes time, which people don't always have, especially when you factor in work, family, commute, etc. Listening to this podcast is like going to a Bible study, but you can do it in the car on the way to work, while you are cleaning your house or while doing the dishes. It is super convenient and he knows so much about the Bible.

Tim Mackie is a self proclaimed Bible nerd and I love all the detail he goes into during his sermons. He breaks the stories down in a way that makes it easy to understand and he also goes into any hidden messages. Tim explains the meaning behind a lot of things in the Bible. He takes a story like Jonah, which is two and a half pages long in my Bible, and talks about it in a 5 part series on his podcast. He goes into so much detail about each chapter of Jonah and what was really going on during this story. Tim is so excited about the Bible and you can tell just by listening to him talk. His excitement is contagious and just listening to him talk gets you excited as well.

As you can see, I listen to a wide variety of podcasts. These are just the ones that speak to me. There are over 500,000 podcasts out there. If you would like to listen to a certain type of podcast, I am sure there is one that fits your exact needs. You can type Christian podcasts, Catholic podcasts, or whatever you are in the mood for, into the search bar and I am sure you will get a bunch of podcasts on a wide variety of subjects. Listen to a few until you find one that speaks to you.

CHAPTER FIVE

The Power of the Holy Spirit

My husband and I moved our family back to the United States in July of 2015. We had spent the last 6 years living in Germany and then England. It was time to come home. At the time our family was struggling. Our boys had behavior issues and Tony and I were not on the same page with parenting, which meant we were also having marital issues. I remember thinking that I needed more God in my life.

I had been working on my relationship with God for several years, and I felt I needed more of the Holy Spirit in my day-to-day life. Whenever I would pray the Glorious mysteries of the Rosary and I would get to the third mystery, the coming of the Holy Spirit, I always wished that would happen to me. I would close my eyes and picture the Holy Spirit coming down and lighting my heart on fire for God. It was as if I could feel the warmth of the fire from the Holy Spirit. I wished for the Holy boldness the apostles had to just go out and start teaching anyone who would listen.

I searched online for a Life in the Spirit seminar I could attend, but I was unable to find any. The Life in the Spirit Seminar is a 1.5 hour long session each week for 7 weeks in which you learn about the Holy Spirit and His gifts. It provides an introduction to the power of the Holy Spirit. I had mentioned to a friend at my church that I would like to attend one of these seminars, if I could find one.

She happened to be at a neighboring church and saw a flyer for a Life in the Spirit seminar. The Seminar was on a weeknight and it began in October and went until December. October is when Tony would go back to Germany to do his 6 weeks of Air Force Reserve time. This meant I would not have anyone to watch the boys. However, this was important to me, so I asked my parents if they could drive up and stay with the boys during these meetings. They live an hour and twenty minutes away, but they agreed.

The seminar was great! I learned a lot about the Holy Spirit and how He shows up in our lives. I learned more about the gifts of the Holy Spirit. I also learned about God's love and his forgiveness. Each week was a different teaching and with each teaching there was a leadership team member who gave a witness about how the Holy Spirit had demonstrated that topic to them. The topics of the seminar were: God's Love, Salvation, The New Life, Receiving God's Gifts, Growth, and Transformation in Christ. I learned a lot from this seminar and I am so glad I was able to attend. What I am most grateful for is that it lead me to my current prayer group.

I became a member of the charismatic prayer group that is attached to St. John the Evangelist Parish in Chelmsford, MA . This prayer group is run by the leadership team that ran the seminar I attended. This is a group of women, and a few men, that gets together weekly to praise and worship God. We begin our meetings with the vision statement of the group: "Our vision is that we be a people united in love and committed to bringing others to a personal relationship with Jesus Christ." What a great vision.

Next, one member gives a teaching/or inspirational talk, using a Bible verse as the launching point. Usually they read the Bible verse and then explain how it applies to every day life. The person who is leading prayer group that week spends time with the Lord and seeks discernment for what they are to talk about. Usually a topic or a Bible verse comes to them and they use that to prepare their talk.

Next, we sing worship songs. We use a worship book called *Holy is the Lord our God*. It has all the words to the songs on several CD's. The leader usually picks 4-6 songs that we will sing throughout the prayer meeting. We alternate between songs, praising the Lord out loud, and those that are blessed with the gift of tongues worship and praise in tongues. If you are new to a charismatic prayer group and are not really sure how to praise the Lord out loud, this group provides sheets with a bunch of praise phrases on them.

Next, the leader for the day says, "Speak, Lord, Your servants are listening," or a similar comment, and we sit quietly and await any prophetic words the Lord may have for us that week. During this time we receive a variety of things. Sometimes people receive a certain scripture verse and so they read it out loud. Sometimes people receive messages, so they share those. We also have some people that receive visions, which they describe to the group. This is my favorite part of the meetings. I love seeing all the ways God shows up for us and communicates to us during these meetings.

Then we spend the last 10 minutes of the meeting praying over any intentions we brought to the meeting, ones that we wrote down and placed in a basket, and ones that we hold in the silence of our hearts. After praying over the intentions, we open the floor for anyone to share any ways God has been moving in their lives. The meeting usually lasts about an hour.

I find these meetings beneficial for many reasons. First, there is something great about praising and worshiping God with a faith filled group of people. Every week, it is as if we can feel the Holy Spirit present in the room with us. We usually have between 12-20 members at each meeting. Imagine all those people praising the Lord and letting Him know how special He is; how appreciated He is; and thanking Him for all the amazing things He does for us.

Praising was not something that came naturally to me. I did not know how to do it, or what to say. However, the group offers praise sheets so new members won't feel awkward or out of place. It is so great. I am sure everyone probably started out using the sheets, but most of them have been there for over 20 years, so they can now praise on their own. I still use the sheets and I find them helpful, even though I do now feel comfortable praising on my own as well.

Second, how amazing! Every week, God shows up to share His word with us. With all the things He has going on, I am still in awe every week that He always shows up for us. This was definitely new to me. I had often spent time in quiet reflection, alone, trying to hear what the Lord wanted me to hear. However, being in a room full of people who were all silently awaiting the Word of God was new to me. It was new to be surrounded by people who were expectantly waiting for the Word because they knew someone would hear what God was trying to tell us. That expectant faith is what I feel I am always reading about and always striving to gain. Yet, each week these men and women sit quietly and just listen.

It is not always the same person who hears the word. It seems many in the meeting have this gift. I wondered if it would be possible for me to hear anything. What I realized was it takes a lot of courage to share something you think you hear. For me, it took a lot of prayer to get over that fear. It is stepping out in faith when you share because you don't always know the whole sentence, or group of sentences you are going to share. Sometimes, you have a sentence you feel God wants you to share, but it is not always a complete thought. Once you start sharing, the next sentence comes. This has been my experience anyway.

I have been in this group for about two and a half years and I just shared my first Word the other day. Well, I had shared a few short messages before that day, but this was the first time sharing when I did not know the whole message when I started sharing. I just felt part of a thought and started sharing and the rest came as I was speaking, one sentence at a time. If I had not joined this prayer group, if I was not surrounded each week with men and women who are brave enough to listen to God and speak out when they think He wants them to, I don't know if I would have the courage to speak out when I feel God is moving me to do so.

Third, sharing your worries and your blessings with a community of believers brings such a sense of comfort and love. Being surrounded by people who believe the same as you do can help you grow in your faith. I have grown so much in the time I have been in this group. They push me to trust more fully and to listen more deeply. They encourage me to step into leadership roles, step outside my comfort zone and be on the prayer team.

That is definitely another way they have helped me grow. Before joining this group, I rarely prayed out loud. I did not think I knew how to pray out loud, unless it was a previously memorized prayer such as the Lord's Prayer. Being in this group showed me you don't have to know what to say. God will provide the words. Just say what you are thinking and no one will judge you.

Another aspect of this group that has helped me grow is their "prayer room." After the regular meetings are over, you can sign up to have individual prayers. This is where you go into a room where two members are waiting to pray over you. Those two members ask why you need prayers. The more specific you can be the better. I know there are things you may not want to tell others, or to even say out loud. That is ok, you can ask for prayers for a special intention. God knows what you need and He knows how to help you.

I have heard on more than one occasion that if you have specific prayers you get specific results and if you have general prayers you get general results. I do not know how accurate this is, but since I have heard it several times, I always try to be as specific as possible when asking God for what I need. Once you are done telling them what prayers you need, they both put their hands on you, if you are ok with that, then one begins to pray out loud and the other prays silently or in tongues for you and the person praying over you. Sometimes they will switch roles, and sometimes not, it just depends on how they feel the Holy Spirit is moving them. I was asked if I would like to join the team that prays over people. I was very nervous, but I definitely wanted to try. It has been a great experience being able to pray over people like that.

One last thing that is so great about this prayer group is that we record all the Words that are given at the meeting. Then we have a discernment team that reviews all the words given each month and discerns which words should be recorded on a book mark to be given out to the group. There are 4 categories for the bookmark. What is God's call that month, what was His proclamation, what was His promise and what was His directive? By recording these on a book mark the words that were given live on and people can go back to them and find comfort in them any time they like.

CHAPTER SIX

The Power of a Group

During a retreat I attended, they talked a lot about how God doesn't call the equipped, He equips the called. This was a new concept for me and I loved it. The idea that all I have to do is be willing to say yes and God will give me all I need to do the job was amazing. At this retreat, they were looking for officers for the regional MCCW board. I had been a part of some MCCW groups at the base level in the past, but I certainly was not on the leadership team and definitely not at the regional level. Those positions were for "holy people," people that were "a lot more Catholic" than I was.

Have you ever felt that way, like you are just not Catholic enough, or just not religious enough? I used to think like that a lot. When they would mention the church had a Catholic Women's Group, I would always think that was for the women who were holier than I was. I felt like I would look foolish if I went because everyone else would know so much more than I did. I was wrong. A group of faith filled women/men is exactly where I belong, and so do you. Everyone there is trying to increase their faith. The people do not know everything, which is why they are there.

Every group that I have joined has always welcomed newcomers and are happy to meet you wherever you are in your faith. Being in a group of people who have a common goal of increasing their faith and learning how to live their faith more fully is a wonderful experience. There will probably be people in the group that know a lot more than you do and there may be people that know less than you do—that is the beauty of the group. How great to have people who have already been where you are, who asked all the same questions, wondered the same things, and can guide you in your journey. Guiding others who are not quite where you are now is also wonderful. They are at the beginning of their journey and you get to watch and help them along the way.

My husband was in the Air Force, and we have been stationed at bases where they had wonderful groups and at bases that did not have any groups. I can tell you, I grew the most when I was involved in a women's group. There is something about being with people who are all striving to live better lives, which makes you want to live a better life. The world has a lot of negativity. It is hard not to give in to it and join in by complaining or gossiping. However, meeting every week with people who are all doing their best to live the Christian life, lifts you up and gives you the strength to rise above the negativity. They remind you of who you are in Christ and that life is a blessing.

The group also gave me strength because we had women of all ages and stages in life. When those of us with little ones or teens would be frustrated, the women with older kids would reassure us we would live through this stage. They would also give us tips or tricks on what worked with their children. When women with grown kids would miss them, they would hold the babies who were at that meeting that day and remember when their kids were babies. This would help them appreciate the stage they were in currently. When someone encountered a problem, everyone was there to pray for them, to offer assistance, and to provide encouragement.

It was not always easy to join a women's group. We moved every few years and I had to look for a new group at each new base. Joining new groups does not come easily to me. Walking into a room full of people I don't know and striking up a conversation is something with which I have always struggled. I have gotten better over the years, mostly out of necessity, but it is still not easy for me. However, I knew that if I wanted to continue to grow in my faith, I needed to find a new group with each move. When I got to Stuttgart, Germany, I found out the chapel did not have a women's group. There was a Bible study that met at people's houses, and I did go to a few of these meetings, but they seemed to fizzle out. After going on the retreat, I realized if I wanted a group on base, I may need to start it. I went to an informational meeting where some of the ladies from the chapel were looking to see if there was interest in starting a group. There was interest, but no one really wanted to lead the group.

You may run into this problem as well. There may be people interested, but there may not be anyone who is willing to step up and say they will lead the group. This is when it is important to know that God doesn't call the equipped, He equips the called. You may not feel as though you could run a women's group, but you can. God only needs your "yes." Once you say yes, He will make you fruitful. He will give you the strength, wisdom, guidance, and everything needed to make it happen. If you want to grow in your faith, more than you ever knew possible, find a group with whom you can discuss your faith, study your faith, and share your faith.

Being in a group that has similar goals to you also helps you to push yourself to be better. In the Catholic Women of the Chapel (CWOC) group in Lakenheath, England, we did the 33 day Marian Consecration together. Would I have done that on my own if they were not all doing it? I would like to say yes, but the truth is I don't know. It required us to read something every day, we had a prayer of the week, and there was a weekly video to watch. I am not sure I would have had the motivation to do all that on my own. I also don't know if I ever would have discovered it on my own. Being around others who are striving to grow, will also introduce you to new ideas.

Being in a women's group increased my faith because they always talked about where they were succeeding and where they were failing. It was so nice to know I was not the only person who failed at times or in certain areas. When a person struggled with something we would all discuss ways to help that person. You might be succeeding where someone else is failing, so you can share what you are doing that is successful in that area. Likewise, if you are failing or struggling in an area, someone else may have an idea that helps you. There is so much out there and it is great to hear from others as to what has worked for them and what hasn't. This can save you a lot of time trying things that may not work and also less time looking for answers someone else has already found.

One of the most important ways that being in a group has helped me is to see that everyone is struggling with something. No one has everything figured out perfectly. One of the enemy's greatest tricks is convincing us that we are all alone in our struggle-that no one is going through what you are going through. No one could possibly understand how hard it is for you right now! He convinces us that our struggles are unique and we shouldn't talk about them to anyone because we would look weak, stupid, or naive. The enemy knows that we are stronger in numbers and if we open up and talk to others that we can defeat any problem.

Lots of people are going through what you are going through right now. You just don't know it because they aren't talking about it either. Honestly, whatever it is you are going through, YOU ARE NOT ALONE! I know it probably feels like you are. That is a lie from the enemy. I went to a conference once and we had to fill out a questionnaire that had about 15 different questions asking about things we had been through. For instance, I have been abused, I have/had depression, I have/had an eating disorder, etc. If the statement was true for you, then you put a checkmark. After we completed the whole questionnaire, we folded it up and passed it down to the end of the row. They were then collected and passed out in a different order. Now you had someone else's paper. To finish, they read each question out loud and if the person on your paper checked off that question you stood up.

The idea of this activity was to show you are not alone. The organizers knew how hard it would be to stand up in front of an audience and admit you have been through these awful things. However, since you did not have your own paper, it was not difficult to stand up because the things you are standing for did not happen to you. The activity was called "Stand up for your sister." It was so powerful to see all these women standing up for someone else. It was also such a powerful demonstration of how many people have experienced the things you are going through.

As you can see, there are a lot of benefits to joining a women's group. In the military, it is much easier to find a group because there is one on most bases. However, you may not be in the military and it may be harder to find a group. Try talking to your priest, minister, or pastor and ask if they know of any women's/men's groups in your area. Look in local church bulletins or on their websites. A local church near me has a women's group called Wine, Women & the Word. This group meets monthly and has guest speakers come in and speak.

If you have younger children, search the *national registry* for a Mothers of Preschoolers (MOPS) group. These groups are usually found at churches and are great for moms with young children. The ones I have been a part of have a nursery so you can drop your young ones off and have some time to focus on you. To find a group near you, go to MOPS.org.

Hopefully, you will find a group near you. If you do not, as was my case from time to time, I encourage you to start a group. You do not have to be an expert on anything. You just have to be willing to give some of your time. Just because you are the leader, does not mean you will have to do all the work. Oftentimes, there are plenty of people who are willing to help out, there just aren't a lot who want to be in charge. Also, nowadays there may be groups online. I am part of a Christian mentoring group called Big Life Mentoring. There are also Facebook groups you could join. It's not always easy to find a group, but I think that is also part of the enemy's plan. He knows we are stronger when we are together and he also knows if it is difficult to find a group, many will give up. I urge you to keep searching until you find a group of people who help you grow in your faith. The journey is so much more fun when we do it with others.

CHAPTER SEVEN

The Power of Confession

Confession is one of the sacraments about which a lot of people argue. Many do not think it is necessary for a priest to absolve you of your sins. I think there is a lot of misunderstanding about what actually happens in confession. The priest is not the one who absolves you of your sins, it is Christ acting through the priest. The priest is a mediator for Jesus. In **John 20:21-23**, "Jesus said to them again, 'Peace be with you. As the Father has sent me, even so I send you.' And when he had said this, he breathed on them, and said to them, 'Receive the Holy Spirit. If you forgive the sins of any, they are forgiven; if you retain the sins of any, they are retained."

Confession is a time when you can tell the priest all that you have done wrong. Sinning is an act against God. When you sin you damage your relationship with God. You may think it is just a small thing, but how many small things have you done since your last confession? It's kind of like a bag you get at the grocery store. You know, the plastic ones that are loaded up with too many cans causing a small hole. What if you parked far away from the store? The farther away you go, the bigger the hole gets. Your relationship with God is like this. Each sin damages that relationship. Each sin brings you a little further away from God.

When talking about confession, many people ask, "Why can't I just confess my sins to God. Why do I have to go to a priest?" My question to you would be, "Are you confessing your sins to God?" Do you take time on a regular basis to assess your actions and confess to God any ways you fall short of how He wants us to live? Yes, you can ask God for forgiveness, and it's great if you do. However, how often do you ask? How often do you take time out of your day to ask God to forgive you for the unkind things you do?

Going to a priest for confession is great because you get to hear someone telling you that you are forgiven for you sins. God no longer thinks about those sins. They are gone into the void forever. The priest can also help you if you are struggling with something. If you find yourself confessing the same sin over and over again, the priest might be able to provide some guidance about how to overcome that sin. It is not that the priest remembers that you are confessing the same sin over and over again, but you could ask the priest for advice about how to overcome that sin. He may see something that you do not see because you are too close to the situation. The priest may be able to provide you with some words of wisdom that you can use to overcome your are struggle. For instance if you are always confessing that you can't forgive this certain person the priest might advise you to begin to pray for God's help in forgiving them, he may also advise you to begin praying for that person daily.

At our church, you can choose one of two ways to go to confession with a priest—through a divide or face to face. Usually there is a confessional booth with the priest on one side and a sitting or kneeling option on the other. The first way, lets you confess your sins through a divider, providing anonymity. The second way lets you face the priest while confessing your sins. You choose the approach that is best for you and that makes you the most comfortable.

If you have not been to confession before, or if you have been, but just did not know about the available tools, I thought I would mention a few to help you prepare for confession. Many people think that they do not need to go to confession because they have not broken any of the 10 commandments and so they are all set. The Church has put out a document called the Examination of Conscience. The one I used for the purpose of writing this chapter is www.beginningCatholic.com.

This document goes through the 10 commandments and breaks them down into smaller actions that make it easier to understand all that goes into each of them. You may actually be breaking more commandments than you think. I know this is not something everyone wants to hear. It is so important that we do hear it though because once you know what you are doing wrong, you can set about to change it. Wouldn't you want to know if you were unintentionally hurting your relationship with your heavenly Father?

For example:

The first commandment, "I am the LORD your God. You shall worship the Lord your God and Him only shall you serve." This is one where it may seem easy to say, nope, I have not broken this commandment. I do not believe in any other Gods. I know the Lord, our God is the only God I serve. However, when you take a look at your life, do others know by how you are living that God is the only one you are serving? "Are you worshiping things more than you are worshiping God?" "Do you pass up going to church on Sunday for something more important?" "Do you worship the TV and movie stars more than God?" "Who and what are you putting first in your life?" "Have you taken care to nourish your faith?" "Have you rejected your faith?" These are some of questions you can find in the examination of conscience.

The second commandment, "You shall not take the name of the Lord, your God in vain." "How many times in the last week have you used God's name when cursing?" "Have you misused things or places that were set aside for the worship of God?" "Have you spoken about the Faith, the Church, the saints, or sacred things with irreverence, hatred or defiance?" "Have you failed to keep vows or promises that you have made to God?" These are all ways in which you may be going against the second commandment and hurting your relationship with God.

The third commandment, "Remember to keep holy the Sabbath day." "Have you missed Mass on Sunday or on Holy Days?" "What about coming late or leaving Mass early each week without a good reason?" No, "I want to be the first one to the parking lot," "I don't like the singing," and "I was bored" are not good reasons. "Do you set Sunday aside as a day of rest and relation or do you do unnecessary work on Sunday?"

"Do you take your children to Mass on Sunday?" I know sometimes it is easier to not take them. I am definitely guilty of this. I know they may fight; be loud; make it so much harder to pay attention; and complain, so sometimes I do not take them. Especially now that they are older and can stay at home alone, I can go while they are sleeping. However, this is not teaching them the importance of Mass. This is not helping them get to Heaven. It is not helping instill The Faith in them.

This is another one I struggle with, "do you knowingly eat meat on a forbidden day?" During Lent Catholics do not eat meat on Friday. This is a struggle for me some years and other years it is not. When we lived in England, the Catholic churches asked all Catholics in England and Wales to abstain from eating meat on all Fridays as an act of penance, not just Fridays during Lent, but all Fridays. This was something Tony and I struggled with. We tried to justify our actions by telling ourselves we are not British, so that rule did not apply to us. That is crazy. It is not as if we were just on vacation there for a week. We lived there for four and a half years. We did not have a good excuse to not abstain from meat on Fridays.

The fourth commandment, "Honor your mother and father." This one may be difficult for some depending on the relationship with their parents. Some people may be thinking this doesn't really apply to them as they no longer live at home or maybe your parents have passed away. This commandment is about more than just honoring your parents.

It is about honoring those who have authority over you. For instance, "have you lived in humble obedience to those who legitimately exercise authority over you?" Also, the examination of conscience for this section deals with the type of role model you are being for your children. "Are you helping them get to the sacraments on a regular basis?" "Have you prayed with and for your children?" I hope you are starting to see that the commandments cover a lot more than they seem at first glance.

The fifth commandment, "You shall not kill." I bet you look at this one and are sure you will not have anything to confess in this category. I mean, most of society does not just go around killing people. However, this commandment does not just address killing someone. It asks questions like, "Have I verbally or emotionally abused another person?" "Have I joined a hate group?" Here is a tough one, have you "killed" someone's reputation? "Have you refused to control your temper ?" Also listed under this one is "Have I been unforgiving to others, when mercy or pardon was requested?" This is a hard one.

I know a lot of people that are holding on to un-forgiveness. I get it, forgiving people is hard! It is especially hard if they did something unspeakable to you and they aren't sorry and are not even asking for forgiveness. Here is the thing that I learned about forgiveness: it is not about them, it is about you. You are not forgiving them so they feel better, you are forgiving them so you feel better. You're not forgiving them because they deserve it, or because it is not bothering you anymore. You're forgiving them because each day you refuse to forgive and hold onto that resentment, it eats you up inside.

I heard a saying once that helped me visualize and understand this so much better. "Un-forgiveness is like drinking poison every day and expecting the other person to die." When you forgive someone you are not saying what they did was ok. It was not. What you are doing when you forgive someone is acknowledging that the event happened, it is in the past and you are no longer going to let it have power over your emotions. You are moving on from it. Forgiveness is about acknowledging what happened, learning what you can from it, and moving forward so you can live your life in the present. One last thing about forgiveness, we are called by God to forgive. It's not just that it's a nice thing to do. God tells us in the Lord's Prayer, "Forgive us our sins are we forgive those who trespass against us."

The sixth commandment, "You shall not commit adultery," and ninth commandment, "You shall not covet your neighbor's wife" are related. The questions for these two are things like, "Have I practiced the virtue of chastity?" "Have I given in to lust?" (The desire for sexual pleasure unrelated to spousal love in marriage.) "Willfully entertained impure thoughts?" "Made uninvited and unwelcome sexual advances toward another?" "Dressed inappropriately?" As you can see, they are not just concerned with whether or not you have cheated on your spouse or coveted (greatly desired) your neighbor's spouse. The commandments are a starting point, but they all go deeper and can be broken down into more specific actions. Actions that, if committed, could lead to a greater sin.

The seventh commandment, "You shall not steal," and the tenth commandment, "You shall not covet your neighbor's goods," are also related. When looking at these two commandments you can ask yourself questions like, "Have I taken something that does not belong to me without the owner's permission?" "Have I envied others on account of their possessions?" This one is one a lot of us struggle with nowadays. It is especially hard with the invention of social media.

There are so many people posting on social media every single day. People post photos of their vacations, of their things, their houses, their food, whatever makes them happy. It is hard not to compare your life with theirs. It is hard not to be envious of the new car they just got, the vacation they just got to go on, or how well their kids are behaved. I have seen a rise in envy over the years and I believe it is because everything is so public right now. In the past if your neighbor got a new car it was in their driveway, so you would see it. Now, if a friend of a friend 6 states away gets a new car you can see it come across your social media feed and then be envious. We need to be really careful about that.

Finally, The eighth commandment is "You shall not bear false witness against your neighbor." This one has questions like, "Have I lied?" "Have I knowingly and willfully deceived another?" "Have I gossiped?" Gossiping is a terrible habit to get into and one most of us can so easily fall prey to. Gossip is so prevalent in our society and sometimes you may feel like if you are not participating in it people will think you are weird, or a goody two shoes. Gossip can kill someone's reputation.

What if someone decides they do not like you and they start a rumor about you. This rumor is most likely not true, but that doesn't stop it from spreading like wildfire. I think we have all been on one end or the other of this scenario while in grade school. It does not feel very good if you are the one the rumor is about. Take a minute before you speak and ask yourself, "Would I like it if someone said this about me?" If the answer is no, then you should not say the thing you were going to say.

I know confession is a difficult topic. I know it is not easy to look at the examination of conscience and think about all the ways we may have harmed our relationship with Jesus. It is also not easy to admit we did some of these things. It is not easy to admit it to ourselves, and it is even harder to say it aloud to someone else, especially a priest. Many people feel that priests must be better at avoiding this whole sinning thing. They must not sin often because of their job. Priests are human, and that means they also sin. There is no perfect human. We all make mistakes. We all mess up at times. Luckily God knew this and gave us the sacrament of confession so when we make mistakes, we can make it right again.

In my experience, looking over the examination before going into the confession and writing down the ones I have committed has helped a great deal. Then I take this list into the confessional with me and I read the list to the priest. Every single time I walk into a confessional I am nervous. At this point, I have been plenty of times, and yet, I still get nervous. It is not a fun experience, but it is a necessary one. I write down my sins because I know once I get in there, I will be nervous and I will probably forget everything I was going to say. I am also an emotional person so I like to have my paper to focus on. You do not have to do this. It is just what works for me. You do whatever works for you.

I have been told another way to go to confession is to focus on what is most impacting you and your relationship with God. So, instead of going through the examination and jotting down everything you think you have done, you would take some time to ask the Holy Spirit to show you any ways you have been hurting your relationship with God. Allow the Holy Spirit to show you the ways you fall short or fail at being the best version of yourself. Bring these things to the priest.

Another option, especially if you have not been to confession before, is to let the priest know that you have not been. Tell him that you want to confess your sins, and repair your relationship with the Lord, you just don't know how, or where to begin. I have heard of people sitting down with a priest and the priest has walked them through confession. If this is the case, you may want to call the priest ahead of time and make an appointment. This way he can set aside enough time for you. The priests are there to help us.

Confession has been a great part of my journey. I know it will probably require a lot of courage to do it the first time, because doing anything for the first time is scary. I urge you to step out of your comfort zone and give confession a try. Outside of our comfort zone is where we grow. There are many benefits of confession that are just waiting for you.

Here are some benefits of confession. Confession helps us to know ourselves better. You have to be aware of your sins in order to confess them. Confession helps you with any persistent sins or habits that you just can't seem to stop on your own. Sometimes you will notice that you are confessing the same thing over and over again. After awhile, you may notice this thing you have been confessing is not as big an issue as you thought it was. Then eventually, you may not even struggle with it anymore. Confession is also a good deterrent to sin. Once you go to confession you are likely to think twice about sinning the next time because your relationship with the Lord has been restored. One way to explain this is to think of confession as a car wash. Once you have washed your car, you are probably more likely to think twice before taking it out in the rain, or down a dirt driveway. Confession is similar to this. Once you have cleansed your soul with confession you think twice before doing something to mark it up.

CHAPTER EIGHT

Pray without Ceasing

"Rejoice always, pray without ceasing, in everything give thanks; for this is the will of God in Christ Jesus for you." **(1 Thessalonians 5:16-18)**

I don't know about you, but I am sort of a perfectionist and rule follower. I like to do things the way they are supposed to be done. I am not a fan of recipes that say add a little of this and a lot of that. I like recipes that lay out the instructions step by step with exact measurements. I do not like to add things that are not in the recipe and I don't like to leave things out. I like to follow the instructions exactly. This is why, when I first heard this passage, I was stuck on the pray without ceasing part. How does one pray without ceasing? What about work, sleep, taking care of the kids? How can I pray all of the time and still do everything that needs to get done for my family? Have you ever had thoughts like these?

Over the years I have heard various ways to pray without ceasing and I thought I would share a couple with you to help encourage you, and to help you realize, especially any fellow perfectionists, you are probably already praying without ceasing. And if you are not already doing it you will see you could easily begin doing it.

In preparing for this chapter, I read a few articles and looked back at some sources I had seen before. They all pretty much agree it is not formal, audible prayer you need to do all the time. It is more of a "heart attitude." **Psalm 34:1** says "I will bless the Lord at all times; His praises will continually be in my mouth." **Isaiah 26:3** says "God will keep them in perfect peace whose minds focus on Him."

Praying without ceasing is about shifting your thought process and turning every day moments into prayer. There was one analogy I found that said, "It's like keeping the radio playing in the background." It is not that you are audibly praying to God 24 hours a day. It is more that you are thinking of God, and he is in the background of all your thoughts throughout the day.

After reviewing all the things and getting ready to write, I reread the verse at the beginning and realized the answer is contained in the 1 Thessalonians verse. Rejoice always, is having an attitude of joyfulness, and in everything give thanks, is having an attitude of thankfulness. How do we rejoice and give thanks? Through prayer! Therefore, effective prayer is a proper heart attitude: a mental outlook of joyful thanksgiving.

Now some of you may hear that and instantly know you are already praying without ceasing. You may know you have a heart for God and you are praising and thanking him throughout the day with your thoughts and words. However, some of you may be like me and may be thinking, yes, that is great, but what exactly can I do to pray without ceasing. I am someone who likes exact steps to follow to make sure I am doing something correctly. This is why I will give you a few examples of ways you can pray without ceasing.

First, I will summarize a video I watched called "3 Steps to Unceasing Prayer," Father Mike Schmitz. If you google this you can watch the video yourself. It is just over 5 minutes long. In the YouTube video, Father Mike Schmitz lists three steps, he learned from St. Francis DeSales, that you could do to transform everything you do into a prayer.

1. **Ask God to be present.** Yes, God is always present and attentive to you, but by asking him to be present you are letting him know you will be present too.

2. **Offer this moment to** God. Offer him all the joy, the suffering, whatever you may be feeling, offer it to God.

3. **Accept** –Resolve to accept whatever comes out of this moment

This will not only transform your relationship with God, it will transform how you live. When you ask God to be attentive to you, you allow every moment to be a sacrament. You invite God into that moment, which makes it a channel of Grace. Then, when you offer the moment up to him, you make each moment a sacrifice. When you choose to accept the outcome, you make every moment a moment of surrender. For instance, you can do this when you go to bed at night. God, I ask you to be attentive to me and I am attentive to you. I offer this night's sleep to you as a sacrifice, as a gift to you and I accept whatever comes out of it.

Another person I admire, Matthew Kelly, in his book *Resisting Happiness*, also talks about transforming every moment into a prayer. He suggests you pause for a brief moment before a new task, or before another hour of work, and offer that work to God as a prayer for a specific person. For instance, God, I offer you this task of doing the dishes as a prayer for my husband, or my parents, etc. He also mentioned if you are studying or reading you could write the initials of those you know who need prayers on the top of each page and before you read or study that page you can offer it up for that person.

There is also something called the Jesus Prayer. This is something you can train yourself to have playing in the background of your thoughts. You can say as you breathe in, "Lord Jesus Christ, Son of God," and say as you breathe out, "Have Mercy on me." This is something you practice and, although it takes conscious thought while learning, it could become something so natural that you do it without thinking. Did you ever notice some things that seem strange at first can become habit? One thing that comes to mind is counting my steps. When I joined marching band, we had to learn to count our steps because while we were marching we were making different shapes on the field. This was strange at first, but 20 years later, I find myself counting steps occasionally.

There are a few other ways you can pray without ceasing. You can begin each day with a conversation with God. You can just sit down with Him and talk to Him as if you would a close friend. Tell Him all about your day, what you have planned and what you are excited about, maybe what you need help with.

Yes, I know God already knows about your day and He knows what you are going to say before you say it. However, there is something intimate about you telling Him anyway. As your day progresses you can continue this conversation and let Him know how your day is going.

You can incorporate prayer into your daily tasks. While you wash dishes, you could pray for a different person with each dish you wash, or you could offer up the task of washing dishes for one intention. This is also effective with any task you do throughout the day, especially if it is a task you do not like doing. Offering up one's suffering for an intention is a wonderful way to pray. If you have something you feel needs a lot of prayer, then you can attach that intention to something you do a lot throughout the day. For instance, you could tell God that every time you wash your hands you are offering it up as a prayer for your children. Think of how many times you would be praying for your children throughout the day.

You could use the time you are stuck in traffic, or waiting in a long line at the store to say a prayer for someone or something. Another way to incorporate more prayer into your day is to listen to music. St. Augustine said, "To sing is to pray twice." I used to put on praise and worship music while I was cleaning or if I was driving somewhere and I would sing along. It made the task go by faster and I was able to turn that time into prayer time.

Another way to pray is to admit it when we mess up, and then move on. Sometimes we spend too much time focused on all that we do wrong. When we confess to God when we mess up, he forgives us, so we do not need to stay in that place of guilt and shame. It is important to take a moment to let God know we are sorry, but he does not want us to dwell there. This prayer does not eliminate the need to go to confession, but it helps us to not hold onto that sin and get stuck there.

Another way to pray without ceasing is to give up worrying. Worry is the opposite of faith. **Philippians 4:6** "Do not be anxious about anything, but in every situation, by prayer and petition, with thanksgiving, present your requests to God." We waste so much time worrying. Next time you want to worry, just imagine yourself extending it up to the Lord our God and letting Him hold it for you. You can ask if you have a role to play, something He wants you to do, but do not take back the weight of that worry. Then start thanking God for who He is and all He has already done for you.

One last way I will share with you is to stop talking once in awhile and just listen. The number or quality of words in your prayer doesn't matter because prayer is about God, not about us. Spend some time just being, simply sitting and resting in His presence. You won't hear anything if you never stop to listen. This is something I feel many of us struggle with. We find asking God for the things we need or even thanking Him for the things He has done for us, comes much easier than stopping and listening to what God has to say to us.

I have always struggled with hearing God, and understanding what that even meant. This can mean different things to different people. Most people do not hear an audible voice, it's more of a thought in their head, or a sense about something. I have come to know that small voice deep inside is the Holy Spirit guiding me. If we never stop to ask God to speak to us, how can we be surprised He doesn't. If we don't step outside the noise and chaos of the world to really listen, then how will we hear Him?

I will end with a quote from Ralph Waldo Emerson "It is not only when we address our petitions to the Deity that we pray. We pray without ceasing. Every secret wish is a prayer. Every house is a church; the corner of every street is a closet of devotion."

CHAPTER NINE

The Power or Retreats

We had just moved to Germany. At Mass one weekend they mentioned that the Military Council of Catholic Women (MCCW) was sponsoring a retreat in Schoenstatt, Germany. The chapel was willing to pay the cost of the retreat for anyone who was interested in going. We moved to Germany in July, it was now October, I did not really know anyone at our new church yet. I usually do not go to things on my own. I feel uncomfortable and awkward. I am shy going up to people and introducing myself, so these type of situations are painfully uncomfortable for me. Not only would I have to go to this by myself, but I would have to drive in a foreign country to an unknown place by myself as well. Luckily we did have a GPS at this point.

I had attended a few retreats when I was a teen and I enjoyed them. I had even been on one as an adult and I enjoyed it. Normally, with all of these things going against me (going by myself, not knowing anyone, not knowing how to drive there, and living in a new country), I would not have gone. However, we moved to Germany when our oldest, Sam was 5 years old, Noah was 3, and Ryan was 1. Life was crazy. We lived in a hotel for at least 10 days with three little ones. Then even when we moved into our house, we had to wait for all of our stuff to make it across the ocean from New Jersey to Stuttgart, Germany. It had been a long summer.

By October, I was ready for a break. I viewed this retreat as a break from all that was going on at home. I think anyone who is a mom can relate. Isn't it strange how we sometimes view time we have without the kids as a vacation, even if it's not. I once had to go to Landstuhl, Germany for a medical procedure. I needed to get one of those x-rays where you swallow something and they take an x-ray every 20 minutes so they can photograph the liquid crossing from one place to another. Landstuhl was a 2.5 hour drive away, so I had to drive up the night before and stay overnight. Then, I had to spend a few hours at the hospital doing this procedure. Most sane people would view this whole experience as an inconvenience. However, moms of three little ones are not always sane. I viewed this as time off—a vacation. I was just picturing sleeping in a bed all to myself. I was giddy about not having to do the bedtime routine that night or argue about brushing teeth. I was so excited that I would get to sleep through the night without having to get up with one of the boys. I was even excited about the procedure because it meant I would get to sit peacefully in the waiting room and read a book in between x-rays. Any other moms know what I am talking about? I love my kids and I love being a mom. I also love the times when I get a break.

Back to the retreat, the fact that the church was willing to pay for it made me think, "You are going to pay for me to go away and stay somewhere for 4 nights?" This was enough for me to get over all my fears of going somewhere alone, driving somewhere by myself in a new country, and all the things I might not normally do. What is the worst that can happen? Even if I just spent the whole time in my room, reading, sleeping, praying, I would go back rested and refreshed. I did not receive any email as to what time I was supposed to show up, but I figured I would head out early because it was a few hours away. I did not get out as early as I would have liked, but that is often normal when you have young children. I enjoyed the ride to the retreat because it was quiet. I was the only one in the car, so I could listen to whatever music I wanted or I could just have silence.

I was late arriving because the main road was blocked off due to construction so my GPS directed me to take a different route. However, it was unclear which way to go and at one point I ended up on a road that had a sign on it and I was not sure what the sign meant. I thought it meant I could not go down that road, but it looked like the way I was supposed to go. I was so frustrated and could not really call anyone for directions as I was in a foreign country and did not know who to call. I prayed God would show me the way and I reminded myself it was not the end of the world and I was a smart person and I would figure it out. I finally made it to the retreat.

I walked in the front door to check in and when I saw I was in the right place I just started to cry. I think I was so relieved to be there! I got to my room and I put my stuff down. I was late so I went right to the introductory meeting. We had an informational session and then we went to dinner. At dinner I sat with a few ladies from Ramstein, Germany. They were very friendly and adopted me into their group for the weekend so I wouldn't be by myself. It was so nice to be included. Everyone at the retreat was so nice. The location of this retreat was the home of the Schoenstatt sisters/nuns. They were so happy to see so many faith-filled women. You could feel the presence of the Holy Spirit throughout that whole week.

During the retreat we had Mass every morning, and then we could sign up for various workshops, depending on what topics interested us. There are usually great subjects at a retreat. Picking which workshops you go to is nice because we are not all on the same journey nor are we at the same place in our journey. You might be really interested in theology of the body and I may want to hear more about prayer. I may want to go to a workshop on how I can involve my kids in prayer, whereas, you may not have kids and want to know more about the saints. We had workshops until about 9 P. M. and then there was a common area you could gather together before bed if you wanted to talk with the other women at the conference. It was so nice to relax at the end of the day and meet the other women. Also, sometimes we would talk about what we had learned that day and what we liked and didn't like.

During these retreats, they always offered a few hours of confession. We would all meet in the chapel and one priest would come up and say a few words. Then, all of the priests (they tried to have any many as possible) would go to separate areas and anyone who wanted to go to confession would get in line. You did not have to go if you did not want to, but when we saw so many other people in line, most of us decided to go. This is so great because some of us had not been to confession in years and many of us had not really been at all in our adult life. What a blessing it was to have the encouragement to go to confession with all these other women. I have been to many retreats since that one and I have heard so many women talk about how great they felt after confession. I have not heard a single one complain or say they regretted going.

Another great thing about retreats is they often have time set aside for Eucharistic Adoration. They would set aside time when the Blessed Sacrament would be exposed and you could go and spend time with Jesus. Often times at the retreats at Schoenstatt they would have Adoration all through the night. So you could just wake up and walk down the hall and be in the presence of Jesus. I will never forget the first time I witnessed Eucharistic Adoration here. The monstrance, the vessel used to hold the consecrated host, was so beautiful. I remember just staring at it and picturing Jesus looking back at me. Even now, 11 years later, I still fill with joy and warmth when I remember that feeling. I felt so loved sitting there. If you have not been to Eucharistic Adoration, go! I will talk more about this in another chapter, but I want to encourage you to try it out.

Previously, I talked about several ways that going on a retreat can increase your faith: workshops, Eucharistic Adoration, confession. Another way retreats can increase your faith is they renew the fire in you for God and for learning about God. If you have never had that fire, go on a retreat. It will give you the spark to get your fire lit. I do not believe anyone could be around that many women filled with love for God and not be changed, even if you are unsure as to why you would want to go. Maybe you are unsure what the excitement is about, or maybe you are like me and think you are just not religious enough for a retreat. I urge you to give it a try. I promise you will be changed for the better. We can all get stuck in our day-to-day routines. Yes, we love God and we do the best we can to pray and thank God for what He has given us. However, a retreat is a time to step away from all the distractions in your life, and recharge your batteries and turn your focus to God and remember how much He loves you.

I want to end by talking about another kind of retreat: a silent retreat. I know I probably just lost some of you. You are probably thinking there is no way you could go on a retreat for a whole weekend and not talk. I get it, I thought the same thing. However, something was pulling me towards a silent retreat. I think the Holy Spirit was urging me to give it a try. I went from Friday to Sunday, so it was less than 48 hours. I really enjoyed it. The one I went to was not structured, we each did our own thing. The only thing that was expected of us was that we go to the initial meeting at the beginning when we met the two spiritual directors in charge of the retreat. Then we each signed up for two sessions with a spiritual director. During these two session I talked about what was going on inside me during this retreat. For instance, did I have any revelations, did I feel called to change anything I was doing, what was I thinking about, did I get any answers to any questions. I talked about how I used the quiet time and what, if any, breakthroughs I had while on retreat.

For example, I had received a Baptism in the Holy Spirit earlier that year and yet I still had not received the gift of tongues, or so I though. While on this retreat, with all the quiet time I had I talked with God about why I hadn't received the gift of tongues. He told me it wasn't Him, He had given it to me. It was me getting in my own way. It was me not believing I was good enough to receive such a gift. I remember how surprised I was to hear this. I remember thinking, "Why would you give me this gift?" I remember God answering, "Why not you?" It was a simple conversation, and yet is was enough for me to go back to the chapel and try to use the gift God gave me. In that chapel at the silent retreat was the first time I prayed in tongues. It was a very special experience and I am not sure if I would have found the time outside of that retreat to quiet my mind long enough to listen to God.

I spent this time reading, praying, and walking around the grounds. Spending time in nature is a great way to connect to God. It's so peaceful and there is so much to be grateful for when you are in nature. The silent retreat I went to also had Mass available each morning. Daily Mass is another great way to increase your faith. There is something different about daily Mass. It is a smaller, more intimate group of people. Also, because it is a small group of people, you actually get to know the people who attend the Mass with you. I don't know about you, but I find going to a church where people know my name, much more enjoyable.

Back to retreats, if you wonder how you can find a retreat near you, google it. I just typed into the search bar of my computer, "retreats near me." I am pretty confident they have retreat centers all over the United States. You could also search, retreat center in Massachusetts, or whatever state you live in. Asking your minister would also be a good way to find a retreat near you. They might have some insight into what type of retreats are around you. However you decide to find one, I hope you do give retreats a try. I think you will be surprised at what a difference they make in your spiritual life.

CHAPTER TEN

The Power of Eucharistic Adoration

Eucharistic Adoration is something I didn't really do before my first retreat. I am not sure I even knew it was a thing. Then when I went to Adoration for the first time, I was not really sure what I should do. I remember being moved by the way the monstrance looked. It was so beautiful. I could not believe we could sit there and talk to Jesus. I know, we can always talk to Jesus, but this was different. This was talking to Him with Him being right there. I picture Him just sitting on the alter having a conversation with me. It is a beautiful experience.

I have had some people ask why I go to Adoration, why don't I just talk to Jesus from wherever I am? If you are thinking this too, I want to reassure you I do talk to Jesus anywhere and everywhere. Adoration is different because you are taking the time out of your busy day to drive to wherever Adoration is and dedicating time to just sit with Him. The best comparison I can think would be visiting a loved one's grave site. Somehow, being there at the grave site, you feel closer to your loved one. It feels as though you are there with them. You can talk to your deceased family members anywhere. So, why do you go to the grave site?

I remember a few very powerful experiences I had during Adoration. One time I was sitting in Adoration and since I had not been before I did not know what to do. I decided I was going to read the Bible while I was there. The one problem, I didn't know where to start. Ok, I thought, maybe I will read about the 10 commandments. Another problem, I had no idea where I would find the 10 commandments in the Bible. I was very new to reading the Bible (if you can't tell). I talked to God and I told Him I had heard of people asking God where something was in the Bible, and then just opening it randomly and ending up on the right page. I decided I would try this. I feel like I had tried it before with no luck, but I tried again anyway.

I asked God to show me where in the Bible it talks about the 10 commandments. I randomly opened my Bible and there they were the- 10 commandments. I could not believe it. It was amazing! I decided to try again. I do not even remember what I asked for next, but I turned to a random page and it was exactly what I was looking for. I was in awe.

I was so grateful. I couldn't believe God, with all that He does, would take the time to show me where something is in the Bible. I was at the gift shop later that weekend and I found a necklace that looked just like the monstrance. It was a triangle with rounded edges, and it had a diamond in the middle to represent the host. I bought it as a reminder that Jesus is always with us. I feel such joy just remembering that time in Adoration.

The next year I went to Adoration, at the same retreat location, I prayed that I could feel the presence of the Holy Spirit. I know He is always with us, but I wanted to feel His presence in a real, tangible way. I was praying and I closed my eyes and I saw this light. It was a white ball of light and it was as if it was dancing on the back of my eyelids. It was so beautiful. I wanted it to last forever. I did not want to open my eyes because I did not want the light to disappear. It did not last for a long time, it was probably less than a minute. I remember just sitting there in awe again that God had showed up.

Why are we always surprised when God shows up? God tells us He will always show up and then we are surprised when He does. Maybe it is because we are used to living in a world filled with humans. Humans don't always show up, we make mistakes, we make bad choices, we hurt people sometimes without meaning to, and sometimes we say we will show up, and we don't. God wants to be with us. If we ask Him, if we invite Him into our lives, He will enter our lives and transform them.

I wish I could tell you every time I go to Adoration I have

experiences like these two. I do not. Maybe it is because I am not asking for this type of experience each time, maybe it is because He knows I do not need it. I am not sure. I do know I enjoy going to Adoration and spending time with God. I like that I can go and be in the same room with Him.

When I first started going to Eucharistic Adoration, I did not know what to do. I thought I would address this since many of you might be in the same boat. To be clear, there is no right or wrong way to do Adoration. God just wants us to be with Him, He does not care what we are doing when we come to be with Him. He would be happy if we just came and sat with Him. In fact, on March 14, 2019 at my charismatic prayer group, one of the ladies received this word, "My children, I love you to be with me. I do not need your effort, I do not need your talents, for I alone will make you fruitful. Just relax, be empty and be with me." However, there are many things you could do if you do not want to just go and sit there and enjoy the quiet.

You could say the Rosary while you are there. Currently when I go to Adoration, I say the Rosary. I have not always done that, but with the craziness of the world today, we need all the help we can get. Many churches have Rosary beads and pamphlets on how to say the Rosary in case you are new to saying it. You can look in the appendix of this book to see how to say the Rosary. There is also the Chaplet of Divine Mercy that you can say on Rosary beads. You will find this in the appendix as well.

Another option would be to read scripture. You can open randomly to a section of the Bible and start reading. If you don't want to randomly open the Bible and are wondering a good place to start I would suggest starting with the New Testament and going on from there. The psalms and proverbs are also good starting places. Wherever you choose to start, read a little of the Bible and then reflect on what you have just read. What does it mean, do you have any questions, how does it make you feel?

I usually take my prayer journal and write to God while I am in Adoration. I write about my day, any things I need help with, any prayer requests, and anything else I want to tell Him. Then I wait and listen to what He has to say to me. I think this is something a lot of us do not do. We talk to God an awful lot, but we don't stop and listen to what He has to say back to us. I have always had a hard time just sitting still and trying to listen to what God has to say to me. Now, instead of trying to sit quietly and listen, I ask God to speak to me through my pen and I write anything that comes into my mind. This has been so great. For me, it is a much easier way to hear what God wants to tell me and I also have a record of what He said since I was writing it down as it came to me. You may be skeptical that this could work for you, but I think if you gave it a try you would be pleasantly surprised at the outcome.

For those of you who would like more structure, I have you covered too. I found this book called "Miracle Hour" by Linda Schubert. I highly recommend you get this book if you get the chance. It is a short book (33 pages) that describes "a method of prayer that will change your life." Linda talks about breaking your holy hour up into 12 five minute segments. The twelve segments are: Praise, Sing to the Lord, Spiritual Warfare, Surrender, Release of the Holy Spirit, Repentance, Forgiveness, Scripture Reflections, Wait for the Lord to Speak, Intercessions, Petitions, and Thanksgiving. In her book she goes into detail on what you could say for each of those 12 sections. I loved finding this book because I am someone who likes to have directions on how to do something. Some people love to be told there is no right or wrong way to do something. I am not one of those people.

Right before finding this book I decided I was going to wake up an hour earlier than usual each morning and spend that time with God. I was very excited about this new idea and couldn't wait to see how much I grew in my faith during this one hour. The next morning I woke up ready to grow. However, there were so many choices for things I could do for that one hour I couldn't decide how to spend it. Some days I would read the Bible, or do my prayer journal, or maybe say the Rosary. Whatever you do is great as you are spending time with God and dedicating time to him. I was struggling because it would take me 20 minutes of the hour to figure out what I wanted to do. I was craving structure and then I found this book at a Life in the Spirit seminar I went to and I was so happy to have some structure.

I know the benefits of Eucharistic Adoration, and I truly enjoy going. I also struggle to find the time to go. I put on my goals sheet (which I fill out each month), go to Eucharistic Adoration once a week. I wrote this for about 4 months before I actually started go. Our days are busy and life happens, and we do not make time for everything. I was speaking to a friend about my struggle with wanting to go, but not actually getting there, and she suggested I sign up for an hour each week. For me, this was a great suggestion, as I do have the time to go, I was just filling that time with less important things. However, if I have a commitment to show up and be there, I will show up and be there.

If you have never been to Eucharistic Adoration, and you are looking for ways to increase or strengthen your faith, then my suggestion would be to give it a try. Many churches have certain times a month they offer Adoration. Some churches have perpetual Adoration, which means they have Adoration 24 hours a day, 7 days a week. You can go onto

http://www.therealpresence.org/states/srtby_st.htm and find where Adoration is offered in your state.

CHAPTER ELEVEN

The Power of Reading Scripture

Reading scripture daily is a suggestion that I've heard a lot over the years. I did not quite understand why we needed to read scripture daily, other than understanding the stories in the Bible. I have read scripture off and on over the years, but it never stuck for more than a few months. Especially all the times I decided to read the Bible cover to cover. Some of those first books are hard to read. There is a lot of genealogy at the beginning and also a lot of the specific rules on various offerings and details for how to build the tabernacle and the offerings tent. I usually gave up at some point.

One time, my friend Genevieve and her husband, Tom, decided to do a Bible study called Read the Bible in 90 days. Each week we would meet and watch a video explaining the part of the Bible we had just read. It was hard to read what was required each week, but I bought the audio version and would listen while doing dishes, cleaning the house, or anytime I was alone in the car. I was happy to get through the whole Bible once. I learned a lot with the study as it was great to have someone explain the various parts of the Bible to me.

I am not sure I still understood how important reading the Bible daily was until these past few years. One benefit to reading the Bible once through completely was I noticed I found the readings in church more enjoyable and more engaging because I had read them before. I have three boys and they are all pretty close in age. They were pretty well behaved in church, for the most part. However, when they were younger it was harder to pay attention because I was keeping an eye on what they were doing. However, once I read the Bible through it was easier for me to pay attention because I had not only heard those stories before, but I had some background information on what was going on in those stories.

Scripture is one way God still talks to us daily. His Word may have been written over 2,000 years ago, but it is still as relevant today as it was then. If you wonder where a good place to begin reading God's word daily is, I can suggest two places, depending on what you are seeking. The first would be Matthew's Gospel, which is the beginning of the New Testament. It is about life after Jesus was born and it has many of the stories you may remember hearing in church. Each year the Catholic Mass cycles through one of the Gospels. Each week at Mass there is a reading from one of the Gospels. There are four Gospels total, but the Catholic Mass only uses three of them, Matthew, Mark, and Luke.

The Gospel of Matthew starts with the genealogy of Jesus. After that, it goes into the birth of Jesus. By chapter 3, you are into Jesus' adult life. It's great to read about Jesus's teachings and the miracles he performed.

The second suggestion is to start with the book of Proverbs. I listened to a podcast once and the woman being interviewed said she took one month and each day she read one of the chapters in Proverbs. Did you know there were 31 chapters in Proverbs? Proverbs is a book in the Bible with instructions on how we should conduct ourselves and what we should and should not do. A chapter does not take long to read and yet it can be very informative.

If you are up for a 31 day challenge, give this a try. Read one chapter of Proverbs each day and spend some time thinking about what the chapter says and how you can apply that to your life. A few of the chapter titles are: "Attitude towards the Lord;" "Attitude toward Fellow Men;" and "The Good and the Evil Way." Proverbs also talks about virtue vs. vice, honesty vs. deceit, and maxims for good living. This book contains some really great stuff. It is perhaps not all stuff we want to hear, and yet it could be beneficial in living our lives according to God's will. You will also find a lot of great one liners you will want to write down and remember. For example, **Proverbs 27:9** says, "The heartfelt counsel of a friend is as sweet as perfume and incense." If you don't believe me, just flip through it and read a few lines here and there. You will be hooked.

When you read the Bible frequently, you get to know God more and more. Each time you read you discover a little bit more about your Heavenly Father. Your relationship with God is similar to other relationships you have. It does not just develop on its own. You need to work at it.

What do you do if you are interested in someone at your work? My guess is the first thing you do is begin to learn as much as you can about that person. You may ask co-workers what they know about them. Maybe you begin to notice what they bring for lunch or what candy they put out in their candy bowl. You begin to watch them and learn what you can about them.

Next, you may introduce yourself to them and begin talking to them. You will most likely begin to ask them questions about themselves, their likes/dislikes, etc. This is all in an attempt to get to know the person and see if you have a lot in common, to see if you get along. You want to see if there is a connection. This process does not stop once you become friends. You continue to get to know each other and learn all you can about each other. All of this knowledge helps improve your relationship. Without the knowledge of what they like/dislike, your relationship is more difficult. What if you brought them candy and they had an allergy to something in the candy. What if you loved cats and they loved dogs. Do you see why it is so important to get to know someone you are in a relationship with?

Why would your relationship with God be any different? God wants to have an intimate and personal relationship with each one of us. We cannot do this if we do not know God and who He really is. Reading scripture gives us a deep and intimate knowledge of God. Scripture is His word to us. It is one way He communicates with us. **Hebrews 13:8** says, "Jesus Christ is the same yesterday and today and forever." If you want to have a relationship with Jesus, then get to know who He is.

Reading scripture also lets you learn about all the things that God promises us. If you know the word of God, you can rely on it when you are struggling. For instance, **Matthew 7:7-8** says, "Ask and it will be given to you; seek and you will find; knock and the door will be opened to you. For everyone who asks receives, the one who seeks finds; and to the one who knocks the door will be opened." My experience in Eucharistic Adoration Confirms this promise!

Jeremiah 29:11 is another great scripture to turn to in times of struggle. "For I know well the plans I have in mind for you, declares the Lord, plans for your welfare, not for woe, plans to give you a future full of hope." If you read scripture daily, or at least frequently, you will find all sorts of verses in your Bible that can help you in times of trouble. **Romans 8:11** says, "The Spirit of God, who raised Jesus from the dead, lives in you. And just as God raised Jesus from the dead, he will give life to your mortal bodies by this same Spirit living within you." What?! The Spirit of God, that raised Jesus from the dead is living within me, within you! That is crazy. Can you imagine how powerful we could all be if we realized that power and gave the Holy Spirit permission to work through us the way He worked through Jesus and the way He worked through the apostles?

We do not know these things unless we read the scriptures. Did you know Jesus told us we could do the same miracles that He was doing? Actually He said we could do greater works than He did. Greater works than Jesus did, can you believe that? **John 14:12**, "Truly, truly I say to you, whoever believes in me will also do the works that I do; and greater works than these will he do, because I am going to my Father." Who wouldn't love to do greater works than Jesus did? How great would it be to be able to go up to a blind man and cure him?

There are people living in this world right now who are doing this. Jesus was not just saying this to his apostles. "Jesus is the same yesterday, and today and forever," **Hebrews 13:8**. He is saying this to us, now, in this day and age. We can do the things Jesus has done, and even more if we just believe. How can you believe in God's word if you have never heard it before? You could read something in the Bible today and for some reason it doesn't really speak to you, and then you could read that same verse in a month or a year and it can really speak to you. That is another amazing thing about the scripture. You get what you need to get out of it. God makes sure that you read what you need to read at any given time.

If you still are not sure about where to start in the Bible, or how much to read each day, I want to let you know there are plenty of reading plans out there to suit your preference. There are Bible plans for 90 days, 6 months, 1 year, 2 years. I am sure you can find whatever plan you want. There are also daily devotionals containing scripture along with thoughts about those verses. A Bible app by You Version offers a ton of Bible reading plans. They have pretty much any topic you can think of and they create a Bible plan around that topic. Some of these topics are wisdom, trust, faith, encouragement, humility, etc. In 2021 Father Mike Schmitz started "The Bible In A Year" podcast. Each day he reads part of The Bible and then explains what he read. It is wonderful. Hopefully, you can still find that on your favorite podcast platform.

Another great place to start reading scripture daily is the readings for the day. Each day the Catholic church has at least one reading from one of the books of the Bible, a reading from the psalms, and a reading from the Gospel. You can go to www.usccb.org to find the reading of the day. There are some publications that have the daily readings along with a reflection to go with the readings. Two I have used before, and really like, are "The Magnificat" and "Word Among Us." Both of these booklets are published monthly. They are great because they have the daily readings, and they have the parts of the Mass as well if you would like to follow along.

CHAPTER TWELVE

The Power of Praise & Worship

I did not grow up listening to praise and worship music. I liked to listen to the radio and I liked to sing along to the songs at church, but I did not own any worship music. One of the retreats I attended, had a Catholic singer, Anne Trufant, as one of the speakers. She had a few CDs on sale and I purchased one. I spent the whole car ride home listening to this CD. The music was so soothing.

I used to love to watch TV. I would get sucked into hours of watching TV. I didn't even have to like the show, it was just an addiction of mine. Once I discovered how good I felt while listening to worship music, I slowly started replacing TV with worship music. I knew I was watching too much TV. Some days, I would watch TV the entire time the boys were at school. They would come home from school and I had no housecleaning or errands done. Listening to music while I was cleaning was one way for me to turn something I had to do into a chance to praise God.

Praising God is so important. He wants us to praise him. The King James version of the Bible mentions the word praise 248 times in 216 verses. There are only a handful of other words used that often. **Sirach 32:13** says, "Above all give praise to your creator who showers His favors upon you." When we praise God we are thanking him for all He has done for us.

In the book, *Opening The Gates of Praise*, Father John M. Capuci talks about 10 reasons why we should praise God. I will not go into all of them, but one that stood out to me was that praise breaks down the walls to receiving God's grace. When I was at my charismatic prayer group one time there was a word given about how we need to break down *our* walls. I asked God silently, "How do we do that Lord?" The very next word given was we can break down the walls through praise. If you want to start to break down some walls, start praising the Lord.

Father John mentioned that many people do not just innately know how to praise; we need to be taught how. There are many ways to praise, but Father John has a specific method, which I found easy to replicate. He recommends that you make four lists. The first is praising God for being God. On this list he looks through the Bible for various names used for the Lord. Following are some of the phrases on the praise sheet that my prayer group uses:

- Jesus, you are the Great Amen
- Jesus, you are the Author of Life
- Jesus, you are the Beginning and the End
- Jesus, you are the Blessed and the Only Ruler
- You are the Great "I AM"
- You are the Just One
- You are the Lord of Lords
- You are the Lamb of God
- You are the Light of the World
- You are the Messiah
- You are the Lord
- You are the Resurrection and the Life
- You are the Way, the Truth, and the Life
- You are the Savior
- You are the Word of God
- You are the Word of Life
- You are the Almighty One
- You are the Hope of the Hopeless

The second list would be of things from your past for which you can praise God. This would include your family and friends, as well as any previous homes you may have had. You can also thank Him for all the experiences you had in the past although some of them may not have been good. A lot of people had terrible things happen to them. I am not suggesting you have to be grateful the terrible things happened to you. Could you be grateful for something you learned from that experience? Is there some positive characteristic which came out of that terrible incident? For example, If you were abused as a child, can you thank God for helping you survive the abuse? Can you thank God for the resilience and perseverance you gains as a result? There were a lot of times when raising my boys was really difficult. There were times when our house was very unsafe. I am not thankful for those behaviors or how scared I felt. I can look back and be thankful that God gave me strength to continue to get out of bed each day. I am grateful God gave me the perseverance to keep trying to get help for the situation, even when I kept running into road blocks.

The third list can contain things in your present for which you can praise God. What do you have right now you can be thankful for? You can praise God for your partner, your children, your pets, your house, your car, your job, and your friends. Are you able to workout each day? Are you able to put food on your table? Some of you may not be where you want to be right now; you may not have all the things you want right now. I get it! I understand that it may be hard to thank God for what you do have when you feel you are lacking what you really want. If this is you, try to think of five things you have right now that you can praise God for. I believe the more grateful you are for what you do have, the more God will want to give you.

The fourth list that Fr. John suggests is those things God is doing in your life right now, while you are praising. Is He curing your headache, is He filling you with joy, what is happening in your mind and body as you praise Him? Try to notice your thoughts and your feelings. Often times during praise at my prayer group, people feel the Holy Spirit all around. Some receive visions while we are praising Him. Whatever it is you feel, see, or sense God doing, praise Him for it.

Although not mentioned in the book, I also praise God for the future, the things that have not yet happened. What is it that you want and have not yet received. God wants us to live with expectant faith. This means that if we ask for something according to His will, He hears us and we should expect to receive it. **1 John 15:14-15** says, "and this is the confidence that we have towards Him, that if we ask anything according to His will He hears us. And if we know that He hears us in whatever we ask, we know that we have the requests that we have asked of Him."

If we have this expectant faith, we can look to our future with hope. If you are still waiting to receive a long desired dream, praise God as if you have already received it! Praise God for giving you the family, or the job you wanted. Saint Augustine said, "Faith is to believe what you do not see; the reward of this faith is to see what you believe." Have faith that, although you may have been waiting a long time, you will still receive that desire you have.

Another book about praise is called, *How to Be A King's Kid* by Harold Hill. If you have not read this book, I highly recommend it. The author talks a lot about how he praises God in every circumstance, but especially when things are not working out in his favor. When it seems like all might be lost and the thing that he thought was going to happen no longer looks possible, he still praises God. Instead of worrying or getting anxious, he starts praising the Lord. He starts telling God that although he sees no solution to the problem in front of him, he knows there is no problem too big for God. Then he thanks God for figuring out the solution and he begins to praise God for being so awesome.

It is easy to praise someone when they are doing what you ask them do. It is not difficult to tell your husband you appreciate him while he is doing the laundry or any other task you are not a fan of doing yourself. It is similar with God. It is not hard to praise Him for the promotion you just received, or for the prize you won in the raffle. It's easy to thank Him and praise Him when your kids have a great day at school or you have an amazing day at work. There are times in our lives when everything seems to be working for us, and in those times, it's easy to praise God and to tell Him how amazing He is and how grateful we are.

What about when life is hard? What about the times when it seems nothing is coming up in your favor? What about the times when you lose your job, your kid gets picked on at school, or you don't have enough money to pay the bills? God is still there in those moments. He is always with you. Am I suggesting you praise God during those hard times, too? Yes. I am not saying you have to praise Him for the hard times, I am saying praise him during the hard times. Although, you can praise Him for the hard time. These are often times when we learn the most.

For example:

"God, I am not sure why our family is having such a difficult time right now. I don't understand why I had to lose my job. I do know that You are an amazing father and that when we ask, You answer. So, I am asking you, God, to help me find another job, a better job, so that I can continue to provide for my family. I don't see how, in this economy, when jobs are in short supply, I could find a job quickly, but I also know I don't have to know because You are amazing and You work all things for my good. I praise you, Lord, and I can't wait to see how You help us out of this problem. You are so good and so faithful to your children and we are so grateful."

In this prayer I am not saying I am grateful to be out of a job. I am not praising God for the circumstance I find myself in, I am praising Him through the circumstances. I am praising Him for being amazing and raising me out of the circumstances. Psalm 28:7 says, "The LORD is my strength and my shield; in Him my heart trusts, and I am helped; my heart exults, and with my song I give thanks to Him." This verse says it all. "The Lord is my strength and my shield" says that God is our strength. When we are weak, our strength comes from Him. He is our shield means that He protects us. "In Him my heart trusts, and I am helped" tells us that if we trust in the Lord, He will help us, He will come to our aid. We do not need to question if He will come, He always comes to help. "My heart exults, and with my song I give thanks to Him" tells us to praise Him and to thank Him.

It is hard to praise God during the difficult times. I am not suggesting it is easy. I am only saying if you can find a way to praise God when you are really struggling, I think you will be surprised how much better you'll feel. I think, even if you are just saying the words and not quite feeling them at first, you will soon begin to feel gratitude. Our minds will believe what we tell them. What is one thing right now for which you could praise God?

CHAPTER THIRTEEN

The Power of The Saints

I love the saints! We can learn so much from them. I think we tend to put the saints on a pedestal and think they were perfect and we can't really learn anything from them because they weren't ordinary people. We think their lives were easy and they didn't struggle with the things we struggle with so we can't relate to them. I am not sure how much you know about the saints, but I am not sure any of them had it easy and I know for sure none of them were perfect because no one on earth is perfect. We are all human, and we all struggle with human behaviors and sins. No matter what you are going through, there is probably a saint who has gone through the same thing in his/her life.

If you struggle with parenting or if you have a child who has turned away from the faith, and/or is getting into all sorts of trouble, look to Saint Monica. She is the mother of St. Augustine. Saint Augustine is a doctor of the Church now, but before the age of 31 he was known for running around with women and having mistresses. His mother did not give up on him and his conversion. She prayed for him and his conversion everyday.

Saint Monica was a Christian, but her parents married her off to a pagan. Her husband wasn't all bad, but he had a violent temper and was promiscuous. Saint Monica's mother-in-law, who lived with, was bad tempered and uncooperative. Even though her husband criticized her for her faith, she never gave up on praying for him and his mother. Her prayers proved fruitful and her husband and mother-in-law both became Christians.

If you struggle with a past that you are not proud of, look to St. Augustine or Saint Mary of Egypt, who ran away from home at

12 and spent years living on the streets as a seductress. She did her best to sleep with as many young Christian boys as she could. One day she went with some men to Jerusalem. They were on the way to see the life-giving Tree of the Cross that was being shown at the temple. She pushed to the front of the line, but when she tried to step over the threshold she could not get in. There seemed to be an invisible barrier preventing her from getting in. She tried several times and the same thing happened.

Mary was too tired to keep trying. She stepped aside and just stood there. She wondered why she could not get in. Suddenly, she felt the word "salvation" and it occurred to her why she was not allowed into the temple. Her unclean lifestyle was the reason she could not enter the holy place. Upon realizing this, she began to cry and was filled with grief and sorrow.

While she was standing there she looked up and saw an icon of Mary, the mother of Jesus. She begged Mary to let her into the temple to see the Tree of the life-giving Cross. She promised Mary as soon as she had seen the cross that she would no longer take part in her unclean lifestyle and she would renounce the world and its temptations. Mother Mary allowed her to enter and once she left, she crossed the Jordon and lived by herself in the desert.

Maybe you are the mother of boys and you are not sure how to lead them with love through all their difficulties. You can turn to St. John Bosco who took care of all the boys in his town. Most of them lived on the streets. He had them in church every Sunday. He never yelled at the boys; he just loved them.

If you struggle to forgive someone who hurt you in unforgivable ways, you can turn to St. Maria Goretti. She was a child of about 12 when her neighbor tried to rape her. She tried to convince him God did not want him to do that to her. He took out a knife and stabbed her several times because she refused to let him rape her. She was rushed to the hospital, and before she died she forgave her attacker.

Do you struggle with a lack of faith? Do your prayers feel unanswered, or maybe you can't even pray right now? Maybe you feel a complete lack of faith, and feel as though there may not even be a God. Look to Mother Teresa. She had a deeply personal encounter with Jesus on a train early in her religious life. She had a vision of Jesus and she told Him that she would do whatever He asked of her.

As time went on she began to feel a deep darkness, almost as if she were in a pit. She did not *feel* the love of Jesus; she did not *feel* anything. Although she was such a powerful ambassador for God's love, she did not feel any of that love. This did not just go on for a year or so; it went on for a very long time. She experienced this darkness for over half her life. She knew there was a God because of her encounter on the train. However, she did not feel His presence for such a long time. She would go to her spiritual advisor and tell him she felt nothing. If you struggle with your faith, you are not alone. Look to St. Teresa of Calcutta to see what she did and how she dealt with those same struggles.

There are more than 10,000 saints recognized by the Roman Catholic Church. That would be a lot to learn if you learned about each one of them. However, if you focus on the saints who had similar struggles as you, that number would be more manageable. I have already talked about a few saints at the beginning of this chapter. There is not enough room in this book to talk about all my favorite saints, so I will finish with three of the saints in my posse.

St. Maximilian Kolbe is my patron saint, meaning he died on my birthday. I was told, whether we know it or not, we have a special connection with the saint honored on your birthday. Before learning this, I had already been introduced to St. Maximilian Kolbe through the Marian Consecration I participated in. St. Kolbe dedicated himself to bringing the whole world to know God through Jesus under the guidance of Mary. He started a newspaper called The Immaculate which was widely distributed throughout Poland.

St. Maximilian Kolbe was not always a well-behaved child. One time when he was young he got into some some trouble at school. His mother told him "She did not know what would become of him." This shook him to the core. He went into their home prayer area and prayed. Mother Mary appeared to him holding two crowns, the white crown of purity and a red crown of martyrdom. She asked him which crown he wanted and he chose both.

He did a lot of amazing things in his life. One of the most amazing was when St. Maximilian Kolbe was put into a concentration camp. One of the prisoners in his cell block escaped. In order to deter that from happening again, the guards randomly picked 10 prisoners left in that block and sentenced them to death by starvation. One of the men they picked was a husband and father and he begged for mercy. St. Maximilian Kolbe volunteered to take his place. It is reported that he sang songs and praised God the whole time he was waiting to die. Kolbe lasted more than 14 days in a starvation bunker with no food or water. The Nazis finally killed him on August 14, 1941, by lethal injection.

Saint Teresa of Liseux is know as the 'little flower.' She was always saying she was too little to do anything on her own. She told Jesus she would do anything He wanted her to do, but she would need Him to lift her up. She said it was as if she was at the bottom of a huge staircase and she was too little to even climb up one step. But if she could climb in Jesus's hand He could be her elevator and lift her to the next step.

A lot of people relate to Saint Teresa of Liseux because it is easy to feel like we can't do much. It is easy to relate to someone who was called to do more, but felt she wasn't capable. Saint Teresa is known for her "little ways" of trusting in Jesus to make her holy and relying on small daily sacrifices instead of great deeds. I think people like this idea because it is a way to holiness through your ordinary life. Saint Teresa did not go on mission trips, she was a cloistered nun, she did not go out into the community to help the poor. She made lots of small sacrifices throughout the day and she did it without complaining and often without recognition.

Saint Rita of Cascia—I just love her! Saint Rita is known as "The Saint of the impossible." Saint Rita wanted to become a nun, but her parents did not like the idea. Saint Rita got married to a man from a prominent family in her town. He was not a nice man at times, his job sometimes got him involved in some shady dealings and she struggled with not wanting to stay in the marriage. However, she kept praying for him and eventually he left that life behind. The two of them moved away from his family and they had twin boys. They were finally living a happy life when her husband was murdered. Saint Rita forgave her husband's attackers publicly at the funeral because she was afraid her sons would seek revenge.

Saint Rita ended up sending her boys away to try to keep them safe. However, they got sick where they were and they died. She was very sad they had died and also relieved they died of natural causes and did not have the stain of murder on their souls.

Rita wanted to joint the Augustinian convent but her applications were always denied. She was not able to join until God stepped in and cleared away any obstacles. Saint Rita once asked for a rose from the garden to be brought to her. The only problem was it was the middle of winter. The person she requested it from went down to the rose bush and to her surprise she found a rose in full bloom. This same thing happened one time when Saint Rita requested a fig from the fig tree.

Saint Rita loved the Lord and she never gave up her faith in Him. She had plenty of heartache in her life and she certainly did not have an easy life. She had plenty of reasons she could have given up her faith in God. She had plenty of chances to blame God for the terrible things in her life. She did not do either of these things. She continued her pursuit to follow His will with all she had.

As I said earlier, I could go on about the saints for an entire series of books. I just love them. I love how much they loved the Lord. I love how dedicated they were to their mission. I know we could learn so much from them if we took the time to read about them. I remember how uncomfortable it felt to read in the Marian Consecration book that we are all called to be saints. I was not sure I was up to that challenge. However, reading about the saints gives me hope if I just keep doing the next right thing, I can get there some day.

What saint are you going to start learning about?

CHAPTER FOURTEEN

The Power of Gratitude

Another great way to increase your faith is to develop an attitude of gratitude. It is hard not to deepen your faith when you start looking at all the reasons you have to be grateful. Most mornings I spend some time writing down 5-10 things for which I am grateful. There are a few reasons I do this. First, it helps me count my blessings. I am intentionally looking for the good things God has brought into my life. These are not usually big things. For instance, I am sure you could put, "my family," "my house," or "my kids/spouse." However, that does not help you see the blessings of each individual day.

The things I put on my gratitude list are much more specific. Every day I try to include things about my spouse and kids, but I try to make them specific. I think about Tony and things he did yesterday for which I am grateful. I do the same thing for Sam, Noah, and Ryan. Some examples of things I write down for my gratitude are:

- Hugs from my boys before bed
- Having a nice conversation with Tony
- Enjoying a cup of tea on the back deck during sunrise
- Playing a game with my family
- Enjoying a nice conversation with family
- Breakfast with Tony

A second reason I take the time to do a gratitude list each day is because I know that what you focus on is what you see more often. Did you ever notice once you notice something, like a new car for instance, you begin to see it everywhere? You might not have ever seen this car before, but once you notice, that is all you see. The same is true for your thoughts. If you focus on how unhappy you are, you will find all sorts of ways you are unhappy with your life each day. If you focus on how everyone else on the road is a terrible driver you will begin to see terrible drivers everywhere you look. However, if you spend your time looking for good drivers-they're everywhere. When you look for reasons to be grateful, you will begin to see them everywhere.

A third reason to develop an attitude of gratitude is that it brings you closer to God. If you spend your days looking for things that bring you joy and make you feel grateful, your eyes will be more open to the wonders that God provides every single day. You may notice more sunrises and sunsets, the beauty of leaves changing colors, the smell of spring rain. Focusing on gratitude is another way of thanking God for all the good that He brings into your life.

Have you ever done something nice for someone, and they don't acknowledge it? If you are a parent, you have experienced this. It's not always that our kids don't appreciate the things we do, they just don't always tell us. Do you remember how that feels? Can you think of a specific instance when you did something for someone and they did not even acknowledge it? It did not feel very good did it? Now, imagine how many things God does for us that we do not acknowledge. I am not saying God feels the same way that we do—He is God. However, if I know how I would feel, that is enough for me to pause sometimes and say thank you and appreciate all He has done for me.

I was listening to a talk on Formed.org one day and I learned about Dayenu. Dayenu is Hebrew and it means, "It Would Have Been Enough." This is a song traditionally sung during the telling of the story of Exodus at the Passover Seder. The song lists a series of kindnesses God performed for the Jewish people during and after the Exodus and concludes each with the word dayenu — "it would have been enough."

The talk I was listening to was called, "Calming the Emotional

Storms: 4 Keys to Finding Emotional Peace" by Dr. Gregory Popcak. In this talk Dr. Popcak discusses how we should each come up with our own Dayenu list. A list of things God has done for us and after each thing write, "It would have been enough." An example of this in my life would be:

- If God had led us to the military and we only did the original 4 years, it would have been enough.
- If God had let us move to Turkey and not found me a job, it would have been enough.
- If He had moved us to Turkey and we only met one group of friends, it would have been enough.
- If He arranged our next assignment and it was not so close to family, it would have been enough.

Ever since the moment I learned about this I thought it was a great idea. I love the idea of acknowledging all the ways that God goes above and beyond what we expect and, frankly, what we deserve. We, as a human race, constantly fail God. We are forever doing the things He asks us not to do. We care more about ourselves than we do about what He wants. Spending time thinking about all the ways He has helped us is a great way to praise Him and thank Him. I am sure if you sit down and think, there are plenty of times where, even if that was all He did, "It would have been enough."

You may be at a place in life right now where you can't see anything to be grateful for. I am writing this book inside of a pandemic and I know people are really struggling right now. There are so many things out of our control. We are not able to see loved ones any time we like, we are not able to go into work, our kids are home from school, we are in constant fear a loved one will contract the virus. There is a lot going on in the world right now. I know life is hard for so many. Let's be honest, it is hard for everyone right now.

I know it seems there is not a lot for which to be grateful. Even if we were not in the middle of a pandemic, everyday life can feel overwhelming sometimes. There is so much to juggle every day. Jobs can be stressful, relationships are hard, children can be difficult, sometimes we have so many things going on at once.

We race out of the house in the morning, then pick kids up at school and then run them to their activities, and then grab dinner on the way home before homework and housework. It is a lot.

Here are some ways you can begin a practice of gratitude. Take a few minutes and think about your day. This could be in the morning and you think about yesterday, or at night when you look over your day. You could do this over your morning cup of coffee, while in the shower, on your drive to work, or whatever works for you. Think about your day and all the things you did throughout the day.

- Did you have any special interactions with your spouse or your children?
- Did anything nice, funny or unexpected happen at work?
- How was your drive to work?
- What was the weather like?
- How was your lunch? Did you go out or did you bring your lunch?
- Did you have to make your lunch or did someone make it for you?
- Did you get to kiss your kids or spouse before heading off to work?
- Did you find time to get your workout done?
- Did you have any nice conversations with anyone today?

These are just some suggestions to help you get started. Your gratitude practice can be whatever you want it to be. Once you start you will see that you have more reasons to be grateful than you think.

What about the person who is struggling to get out of bed? A lot of people struggle with depression and anxiety. If this is you, the previous questions might not be the ones for you. If you struggle to get out of bed and really do not see any reason to be grateful, because life seems so overwhelming, here are a few questions for you:

- Did I get out of bed today?
- Did I make my bed this morning?
- Was I able to get dressed today?
- Did I eat something today?

- Did I take care of myself today?
- Did I do something, even though I didn't really want to?
- Was I able to feed my kids today?

At a conference I attended the speaker talked about how badly she was depressed. She had constant pain and could not see how anything would get better. What helped her was to go outside for a few minutes each morning and try to be grateful for everything she saw and felt. Following are some examples:

- I am grateful for the sun shining on my face.
- I am grateful for the cool/warm breeze.
- I am grateful for the birds singing.
- I am grateful for the green grass.
- I am grateful that it is not raining.
- I am grateful for the rain as the grass needs it.

If you are struggling right now, I urge you to try practicing gratitude for 30 days and see if it helps. Doing so does not take a lot of time and it can make a world of difference. You do not have to be struggling to see the benefits of gratitude. Everyone will see benefits in their life if they begin to have an attitude of gratitude. Take a minute now and think of 5 things for which you are grateful. How could you incorporate gratitude into your day?

CHAPTER FIFTEEN

The Power of a Spiritual Director

If you are like most people you may not have any idea of what a spiritual advisor/director does. I am sure you have some inkling as you can imagine just by the name that they are someone who advises you in your faith—someone who directs you on your faith journey. I had heard of spiritual directors and advisors, but I never considered getting one. I knew for sure they were for "holy people" and that I was not "holy enough" to need or deserve one of those. I laugh when I think back, as it never occurred to me they could help me become more holy. It's like thinking I don't need a music lesson because I am not very good at playing an instrument. That is when you need the music lessons the most. I am not sure why this never occurred to me.

I read a book a few years ago called *Resisting Happiness*, by Matthew Kelly. If you have not read it, you should; it's great. He talked about the idea of getting a spiritual advisor. He likened it to getting a coach if you are an athlete. He mentioned how his dad always told him and his brothers to "listen to the coach." When he asked his dad why his dad said, "Because nobody ever achieves excellence at anything without coaching." You can teach yourself to be really good at a lot of things, especially if you already have a talent in some area. However, if you truly want to be excellent, get coaching from someone who can take you to the next level.

I had never thought about my faith in this way. I have thought of it in the sense that I do want to be the best Catholic I can be. I joined Bible studies and read spiritual books to help me grow in my faith. I just never thought of getting a spiritual director to help me on my path. I do not think a lot of people think of this option. There could be many reasons why people do not feel they want to seek out a spiritual director.

Maybe some of those reasons are holding you back. They don't need to do so. Maybe you don't know what to expect. I understand this one, because I was nervous to attend my first session, for exactly this reason. However, when you first call to make the appointment, you can ask the director what to expect for your first visit or what happens during a typical session. This way, you have some idea of what you are walking into.

I was also afraid that I did not know very much about our faith. I was worried that within 5 minutes of talking with me, the advisor would figure out that I was a fraud. The advisor would learn that I attend Mass, try to do Bible studies and learn about our faith, and yet I don't really know anything. Some of you know exactly what I am talking about. Those fears are the enemy talking. No one in the business of spiritual direction is going to judge what you do or do not know. If you are seeking out spiritual direction, you are seeking ways to be better; no one will judge you for that!

Another thing I worried about, which may seem strange, was would he or she ask me to do something I did not want to do. For instance, they might tell me to say the Rosary every day, or to attend Mass every day. There is nothing wrong with either of these things and I have done them both at various times over the years. However, I was afraid there could be some work involved and I was unsure how I felt about that.

First, in my experience the spiritual director does not tell you what to do. They may suggest things that can help you in one area or another, but I do not think they will mandate anything.

Second, it should be work. God made us in his image and likeness, and yet we are human and struggle with our humanity. Becoming an exceptional Christian requires work; just like becoming a great wife, husband, worker, etc., requires work. That is good news. We do not grow in easy times. We grow and change in the hard times. We grow when we step out of our comfort zone and work on things.

Another potential roadblock could be you do not know where to find a spiritual director. This one roadblock used to be enough for me to stop trying. I would tell myself I had no idea where to find one and so I shouldn't even try. Or, I would put it on my list of things I would do "someday." However, since I had no idea where to start, I was never going to get to it. Do you ever feel like that? Do you ever have something you want to do, but have no idea where to even begin, so you don't?

Let me start you off with some ideas of how to start. This way you will hopefully not get stuck before you even start. The first thing to do is pray. Ask God to lead you to the spiritual director that He has planned for you. Then, be on the lookout. When I decided to seek out a spiritual director, I had no idea where to look. Then all of the sudden there was an ad in our church bulletin a few weeks later for a woman who was studying to be a spiritual director and needed practice clients. I called right away. Unfortunately she had already found her practice client. However, she pointed me to the deacon's wife, who was available to be my spiritual director.

You can also ask your priest. I am not saying you should go up to your priest and ask him to be your spiritual director—they already have a lot on their plate. I would suggest you speak to him and let him know you are looking for, or have been thinking about getting a spiritual director. They probably know if someone in your parish fills this role. Aso, if they had the time and wanted to do it, they could offer their services.

You could also ask around to other people you know at your church. They may know of someone who does spiritual direction. Some local diocese, keep a list of spiritual directors. You could also search online for some. I just googled it and found a website for an organization called Spiritual Directors International. I am sure there are other websites as well. (www.sdiworld.org)

Another option is to ask someone you look up to or admire at your church. There are likely a lot of people in your church farther along on their spiritual journey. Just as I am sure there are a lot of people not as far as you. Those who are farther along can guide us on our journeys. They have already been where you are, even if it is not exactly the same scenario, and they have made it through. They can be extremely helpful in showing or telling you what worked for them and what did not work.

A final place I will suggest that you look would be at any religious organizations in your area. Sometimes priests who are in a religious order and not a parish priest may have the time to be your spiritual director. Also there are many religious sisters, deacons, and other lay people who may be a great fit for you.

The person helping you does not necessarily have to be a certified spiritual director. The purpose is to find someone who can listen to what is going on in your life, hold a mirror up and help you to see where the Holy Spirit is moving in your life. Father Mike Schmitz said, "Holiness is saying yes to the will of the Father." If you can find someone to help you see where God seems to be calling you, that is great. Who do you know who could be your spiritual director? Do you look up to any people in your church who might be willing to mentor you?

CONCLUSION

I hope this book has provided several ideas about how to deepen your faith. Remember, to set yourself up for success, try one new thing at a time. This is super hard for me. When I hear a list of things that I can do to improve an area, I want to start them all immediately. If one could help me, then five could really help. However, the likelihood that I am going to keep up five new habits is not very good. Everything can change, just not all at the same time. You can add five new habits into your daily routine, it just helps if you do it one at a time.

Try out one new thing for a month and see if you like it. Check and see if it is something you enjoy doing and if it bears fruit. We all have busy lives. There are usually a million things pulling at our attention throughout the day. You will be surprised at how much calmer your life will feel just by adding in one new thing that focuses on God.

Often times we feel we don't have time to pray. We feel as though we can't fit one more thing into our already overbooked schedule. I get it. I feel that way sometimes. If this is you right now, know that you are not alone. Also want you to know that you don't *have* to fit one more thing into your schedule. You can combine prayer with something you are already doing. What about saying a prayer while you drive to work? Add some prayer time when you shower. You can include some of these habits without adding more time to your schedule.

A really short prayer that I learned from my mentor & podcast host Pamela Crim is the four-sentence prayer. This prayer is so short you could even do it will you are waiting in the grocery store line:

1. What are you thankful for?
2. Confess where you messed up and ask for forgiveness.
3. What are you worried about?
4. Ask for help.

For example, Thank you that I can afford to shop. Forgive me for not picking up the grapes I dropped in the store. Father, I'm afraid for my kid with all the school violence. Please keep them safe. If you take a few moments to answer these questions on a daily basis, you will see results.

I know that starting new habits is difficult. We all have the best of intentions and then life happens. We get on a roll and then a vacation comes up, we get sick, or something else gets us off track. That is ok! It happens to all of us. Just don't give up; keep trying again and again. God wants our persistence not our perfection. In 2 Corinthians 12:9 God said, "My grace is sufficient for you, for my power is made perfect in weakness." God is made perfect in our weakness. To me, this was great to hear. It removes the pressure on me to try and be perfect. We are all human and perfection is not in our nature. It is nice to know that when we fall short, we can rely on God's grace to get us through.

I would like to explain a few things I learned about starting new habits. First, putting them on your schedule helps to ensure that they actually happen. I can say I am going to pray every day for 10 minutes. However, if I don't take a moment to think about I am going to fit that in during the day, it probably won't happen. Second, doing the new habit at the same time every day is a great way to ensure that you do it. Third, anchoring that habit with an already existing habit helps. For instance, pray right after you brush your teeth. Brushing your teeth will become the habit that tells your mind that prayer is next.

If the habit you want to include in your day or week is something like Eucharistic Adoration or Confession, then scheduling it will be particularly important. These options may only be available at certain times. I tried to get in the habit of going to Adoration once a week, but it was not happening. Finally, someone mentioned that if I signed up for an hour time slot, then I would have that commitment and I would need to show up. That was just what I needed. A lot of us struggle with making a commitment to ourselves. However, we always show up when others are counting on us. Sometimes, having accountability with someone else can be just what you need to start a new habit. Is there someone that you could arrange to meet at Adoration or confession? Maybe you go out for a quick cup of coffee afterwards?

I am so excited that you are on this journey. Reading this book is a great step forward. The next step is to pick a habit and incorporate it into your routine. Whatever habit you decide to pick, I know it is going to be fruitful. The fact that you are actively seeking a deeper relationship with our heavenly Father is powerful. Let me end with a message that was given to my prayer group.

Believe that you can make a difference when I am there. Believe that I lead each step of the way. Each step that I lead you is a step to my kingdom. Continue to believe, continue to trust, continue to show my love to one and all. All can be because I am with you each and every day.

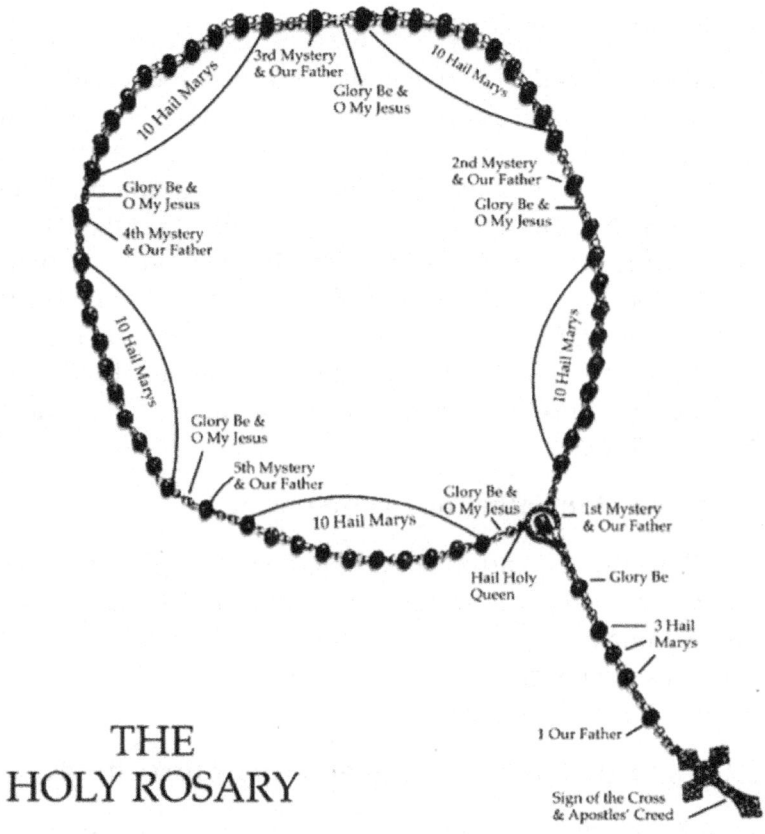

THE
HOLY ROSARY

How to say the Rosary:

1.) Begin by making the sign of the cross and praying the Apostle's Creed while you hold onto the crucifix.

Sign of the cross: In the name of the Father, and of the Son, and of the Holy Spirit. Amen.

Apostles' Creed: I believe in God, the Father almighty, Creator of heaven and earth, and in Jesus Christ, His only Son, our Lord, who was conceived by the Holy Spirit, born of the Virgin Mary, suffered under Pontius Pilate, was crucified, died, and was buried; He descended into hell; on the third day He rose again from the dead; He ascended into heaven, and is seated at the right hand of God the Father almighty; from there He will come to judge the living and the dead. I believe in the Holy Spirit, the holy Catholic Church, the communion of saints, the forgiveness of sins, the resurrection of the body, and life everlasting. Amen.

2.) Pray 1 Our Father on the first bead.

Our Father, Who art in heaven, hallowed be Thy name; Thy kingdom come; Thy will be done on earth as it is in heaven. Give us this day our daily bread, and forgive us our trespasses as we forgive those who trespass against us, and lead us not into temptation, but deliver us from evil, Amen.

3.) Pray 1 Hail Mary on each of the next three beads

Hail Mary, full of grace, the Lord is with thee. Blessed art thou amongst women, and blessed is the fruit of thy womb, Jesus. Holy Mary, Mother of God, pray for us sinners, now and at the hour of our death, Amen.

4.) On the next bead, pray the Glory Be.

Glory be to the Father, and to the Son, and to the Holy Spirit, as it was in the beginning, is now, and ever shall be, world without end. Amen.

5.) On each large bead, read one of the mysteries and then

pray 1 Our Father.

The Joyful Mysteries: The Annunciation, The Visitation, The Nativity, The Presentation of the Lord, & The Finding in the Temple.

The Luminous Mysteries: The Baptism of Jesus in the Jordan, The Wedding at Cana, Jesus Proclaims God's Kingdom, The Transfiguration of Jesus, & The Institution of the Eucharist.

The Sorrowful Mysteries: The Agony of Jesus in the Garden, Jesus is Scourged at the Pillar, Jesus is Crowned with Thorns, Jesus Carries the Cross, Jesus Dies upon the Cross.

The Glorious Mysteries: Jesus Rises from the Dead, Jesus Ascends into Heaven, The Coming of the Holy Spirit on Mary and the Apostles, The Assumption of Mary to Heaven, The Coronation of Mary as Queen.

Our Father, Who art in heaven, hallowed be Thy name; Thy kingdom come; Thy will be done on earth as it is in heaven. Give us this day our daily bread, and forgive us our trespasses as we forgive those who trespass against us, and lead us not into temptation, but deliver us from evil, Amen.

6.) **On each smaller bead, pray 1 Hail Mary.**

Hail Mary, full of grace, the Lord is with thee. Blessed art thou amongst women, and blessed is the fruit of thy womb, Jesus. Holy Mary, Mother of God, pray for us sinners, now and at the hour of our death, Amen.

(6a) **End with a Glory Be and the Fatima Prayer.**

Glory be to the Father, and to the Son, and to the Holy Spirit, as it was in the beginning, is now and ever shall be, world without end. Amen.

Fatima Prayer: Oh my Jesus, forgive us our sins; save us from the fires of hell. Lead all souls to Heaven, especially those most in need of Your Mercy.

Once you complete a mystery, (the Our Father, the 10 Hail Mary's, the Glory Be and the Fatima Prayer), you have completed a decade of the Rosary. There are 5 decades.

6.) **After finishing the last decade, pray the Hail Holy Queen and the Final Prayer.**

Hail, holy Queen, Mother of mercy, hail, our life, our sweetness, and our hope. To you we cry, the children of Eve; to you we send up our sighs, mourning, and weeping in this land of exile. Turn, then, most gracious Advocate, your eyes of mercy toward us; lead us home at last, and show us the blessed fruit of your womb, Jesus: O clement, O loving, O sweet Virgin Mary.

~Pray for us, O holy Mother of God.

~That we may be made worthy of the promises of Christ.

Final Prayer: O God, whose Only Begotten Son, by his Life, Death, and Resurrection, has purchased for us the rewards of eternal life, grant, we beseech thee, that while meditating on these mysteries of the most holy Rosary of the Blessed Virgin Mary, we may imitate what they contain and obtain what they promise, through the same Christ our Lord. Amen.

Catherine J. Duggan

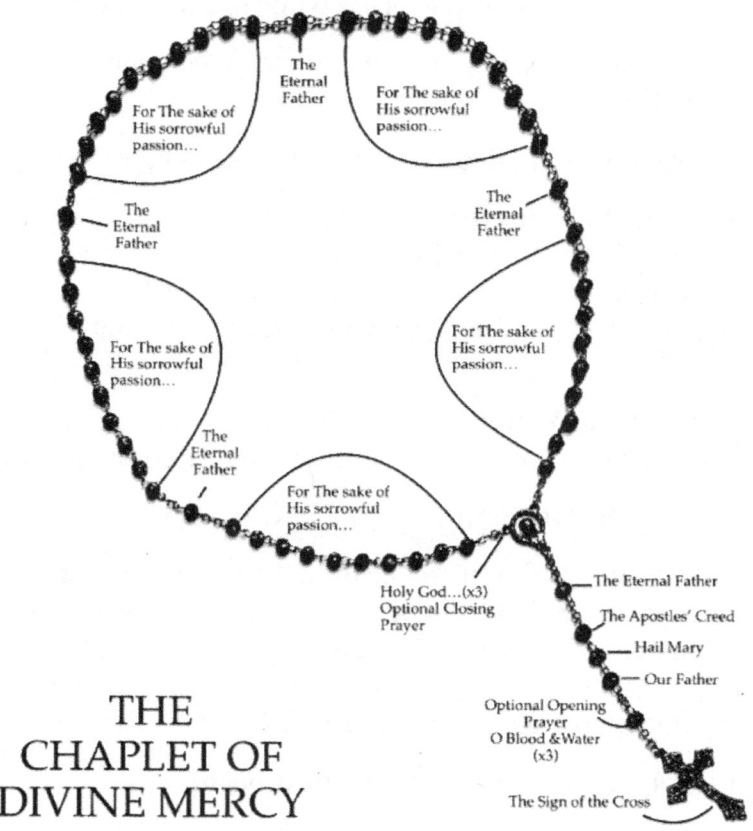

THE
CHAPLET OF
DIVINE MERCY

How to say the Chaplet of Divine Mercy:

1.) Make the sign of the Cross while holding the crucifix.

Sign of the Cross: In the name of the Father, and of the Son, and of the Holy Spirit. Amen.

2.) Optional Opening Prayers while holding the first bead.

St. Faustina's Prayer for Sinners: "You expired, Jesus, but the source of life gushed forth for souls, and the ocean of mercy opened up for the whole world. O Fount of Life, unfathomable Divine Mercy, envelop the whole world and empty Yourself out upon us

O Blood and Water, which gushed forth from the Heart of Jesus as a fount of mercy for us, I trust in You! (Repeat three times)

3.) Pray the Our Father on the next bead.

Our Father, Who art in heaven, hallowed be Thy name; Thy kingdom come; Thy will be done on earth as it is in heaven. Give us this day our daily bread, and forgive us our trespasses as we forgive those who trespass against us, and lead us not into temptation, but deliver us from evil, Amen.

4.) Pray the Hail Mary on the next bead.

Hail Mary, full of grace. The Lord is with thee. Blessed art thou amongst women, and blessed is the fruit of thy womb, Jesus. Holy Mary, Mother of God, pray for us sinners, now and at the hour of our death, Amen.

5.) Pray The Apostles' Creed on the next bead.

Apostles' Creed: I believe in God, the Father almighty, Creator of heaven and earth, and in Jesus Christ, His only Son, our Lord, who was conceived by the Holy Spirit, born of the Virgin Mary, suffered under Pontius Pilate, was crucified, died, and was buried; He descended into hell; on the third day He rose again from the dead; He ascended into heaven, and is seated at the right hand of God the Father almighty; from there He will come to judge the living and the dead. I believe in the Holy Spirit, the holy Catholic Church, the communion of saints, the forgiveness of sins, the resurrection of the body, and life everlasting. Amen.

6.) Pray The Eternal Father on the 5 large beads

Eternal Father, I offer you the Body and Blood, Soul and Divinity of Your Dearly Beloved Son, Our Lord, Jesus Christ, in atonement for our sins and those of the whole world.

7.) Pray the following on each of the 10 small beads

For the sake of His sorrowful Passion, have mercy on us and on the whole world.

8. Repeat for the remaining decades

Saying the **"Eternal Father"** on the large bead and then 10 **"For the sake of His sorrowful Passion"** on the following smaller beads.

9. Conclude with Holy God (Repeat three times)

Holy God, Holy Mighty One, Holy Immortal One, have mercy on us and on the whole world.

10. Optional Closing Prayers

Eternal God, in Whom mercy is endless and the treasury of compassion — inexhaustible, look kindly upon us and increase Your mercy in us, that in difficult moments we might not despair nor become despondent, but with great confidence submit ourselves to Your holy will, which is Love and Mercy itself.

The Litany of Trust:

From the belief that I have to earn Your love... Deliver me, Jesus.

From the fear that I am unlovable... Deliver me, Jesus.

From the false security that I have what it takes... Deliver me, Jesus.

From the fear that trusting you will leave me more destitute... Deliver me, Jesus.

From all suspicion of your words and promises... Deliver me, Jesus.

From the rebellion against childlike dependency on You... Deliver me, Jesus.

From refusals and reluctances in accepting Your will... Deliver me, Jesus.

From anxiety about the future... Deliver me, Jesus.

From resentment or excessive preoccupation with the past... Deliver me, Jesus.

From restless self-seeking in the present moment... Deliver me, Jesus.

From disbelief in Your love and presence... Deliver me, Jesus.

From the fear of being asked to give more than I have... Deliver me, Jesus.

From the belief that my life has no meaning or worth... Deliver me, Jesus.

From the fear of what love demands... Deliver me, Jesus.

From discouragement... Deliver me, Jesus.

That You are continually holding me, sustaining me, loving me... Jesus, I trust in You.

That Your love goes deeper than my sins and failings and transforms me... Jesus, I trust in You.

That not knowing what tomorrow brings is an invitation to lean on You... Jesus, I trust in You.

That You are with me in my suffering... Jesus, I trust in You.

That my suffering, united to Your own, will bear fruit in this life and the next... Jesus, I trust in You.

That You will not leave me orphan, that You are present in Your Church... Jesus, I trust in You.

That Your plan is better than anything else... Jesus, I trust in You.

That You always hear me and in Your goodness always respond to me... Jesus, I trust in You.

That You give me the grace to accept forgiveness and to forgive others... Jesus, I trust in You.

That You give me all the strength I need for what is asked... Jesus, I trust in You.

That my life is a gift... Jesus, I trust in You.

That You will teach me to trust You... Jesus, I trust in You.

That You are my Lord and my God... Jesus, I trust in You.

That I am Your beloved one... Jesus, I trust in You.

Written by Sr. Faustina Maria Pia, Sisters of Life

Litany of Humility

O Jesus, meek and humble of heart, hear me.

From the desire of being esteemed, deliver me, Jesus.

From the desire of being loved, deliver me, Jesus.

From the desire of being extolled, deliver me, Jesus.

From the desire of being honored, deliver me, Jesus.

From the desire of being praised, deliver me, Jesus.

From the desire of being preferred to others, deliver me, Jesus.

From the desire of being consulted, deliver me, Jesus.

From the desire of being approved, deliver me, Jesus.

From the fear of being humiliated, deliver me, Jesus.

From the fear of being despised, deliver me, Jesus.

From the fear of suffering rebukes, deliver me, Jesus.

From the fear of being calumniated, deliver me, Jesus.

From the fear of being forgotten, deliver me, Jesus.

From the fear of being ridiculed, deliver me, Jesus.

From the fear of being wronged, deliver me, Jesus.

From the fear of being suspected, deliver me, Jesus.

That others may be loved more than I, Jesus, grant me the grace to desire it.

That others may be esteemed more than I, Jesus, grant me the grace to desire it.

That, in the opinion of the world, others may increase and I may decrease, Jesus, grant me the grace to desire it.

That others may be chosen and I set aside, Jesus, grant me the grace to desire it.

That others may be praised and I go unnoticed, Jesus, grant me the grace to desire it.

That others may be preferred to me in everything, Jesus, grant me the grace to desire it.

That others may become holier than I, provided that I may become as holy as I should, Jesus, grant me the grace to desire it.

About The Author

Catherine is a certified life coach & spiritual coach, through the Life Purpose Institute. She has a M. Ed in Special Education and is married with three sons. Her husband is retired from the Air Force so they have lived in three different states and three different countries. This gave her the opportunity to be a part of various Christian Women's Groups over the years. Some of these include MOPS (Mothers with Pre-Schoolers), the MCCW (Military Council of Catholic Women), CWOC (Catholic Women of the Chapel), home Rosary Groups, Bible studies, and prayer groups. She is a life long learner and especially loves learning about the Catholic faith.

God has always been a source of strength for Catherine. Her parents set a wonderful example by living out their faith. When difficulties arose in life, as they do for all of us, she learned to lean into her faith and trust in the Lord to help during the tough times. Catherine always knew God was there with her, even when it was difficult to understand why it was all happening. In her heart, she knew God was looking out for her family.

Her dream is to be a light in the darkness of this world and to help as many people as she can to deepen their personal relationships with Jesus Christ and live their lives more fully. To help achieve this dream Catherine has a daily devotional podcast called *Walk Boldly with Jesus*, which can be found on most podcast platforms and also on YouTube.

For more information or to get in touch with Catherine go to her website findingtruenorthcoaching.com.

Made in United States
North Haven, CT
20 August 2024

56313907R00065